WINDOWS XP
TIPS & TRICKS

STUART YARNOLD

in easy steps

BARNES
&NOBLE
BOOKS
NEW YORK

In easy steps is an imprint of Computer Step
Southfield Road . Southam
Warwickshire CV47 0FB . United Kingdom
www.ineasysteps.com

This edition published for Barnes & Noble Books, New York
FOR SALE IN THE USA ONLY
www.bn.com

Notice of Liability
Every effort has been made to ensure that this book contains
accurate and current information. However, Computer Step and the
author shall not be liable for any loss or damage suffered by readers
as a result of any information contained herein.

Trademarks
Microsoft® and Windows® are registered trademarks of Microsoft
Corporation. All other trademarks are acknowledged as belonging to
their respective companies.

Printed and bound in the United Kingdom

ISBN 0-7607-4793-8

Contents

3 System Customization   59

4 Information   77

5 Email   89

Performance

This chapter shows you how to get the best out of your PC in terms of speed and efficiency.

Covers

Chapter One

Introduction

Windows is by far the most popular operating system in the world today, for reasons that are not too hard to understand.

No other system comes close to matching it in terms of sheer "user friendliness". It's widely available, easy to install and configure, and although earlier versions were prone to crashing, Windows 98 and onwards have proved to be more stable and reliable. XP takes this several stages further and is the most reliable and crash-proof system Microsoft has produced. Furthermore, virtually all software these days is written for Windows or has a Windows version.

Windows XP's architecture is based on Windows 2000, which is Microsoft's professional and premier operating system. As such, it is radically different in many ways from Windows ME/98/95. Many tricks and tweaks that worked with these older systems won't with XP.

One of the main reasons for Windows' enduring popularity is the ease with which its default settings can be tweaked and adjusted. Most people though, simply have no idea of the extent to which they can set up their PC to suit their own particular purposes and boost its overall efficiency.

Something else that must be said is that the computer manufacturers all too often deliver PCs in a less than optimum condition, leaving it to the unfortunate user to correct basic setting up errors. If, as is often the case, the user knows little or nothing about computers, he or she will very often operate the PC for months or even years, never knowing that they are not getting the best out of it.

The tips and tricks in this book are designed to work with Windows XP Home Edition and Professional. Some will work with other Windows versions, some will not.

The aim of this book is to help people like this realize what they can, and indeed should, achieve with their PC. A computer is a finely tuned machine, much like a Formula One racing car, and to keep it running at peak performance, it needs constant care and attention. There are any number of tweaks and adjustments that can be made to help achieve this and some of these are detailed in Chapter One.

Most people like to customize their computers, both to complement their own personality and also to achieve specific tasks. In common with previous versions, XP provides numerous ways to do so. Chapters Two and Three demonstrate a range of tips to help you personalize your PC.

More so than any other Windows version, XP is a positive mine of information, both about itself and computing in general. Many commonplace problems can be easily and quickly solved by making use of this information. Learn how in Chapter Four.

A common use of computers these days is to access email and the Internet. In Chapters Five and Six we'll see how to get the best out of these popular applications with, for example, tips on how to achieve reliable connections and downloads. Viruses are another aspect of email that need to be considered and you will learn how to identify potentially dangerous messages before they can cause any damage to your computer.

Security can be an important issue, especially in a multi-user environment, and you will discover in Chapter Seven that XP provides a number of ways to safeguard and hide sensitive data. The Internet can be a risky place for children and XP does provide the means to limit the potential dangers.

Installing and setting up software can sometimes be far from straightforward including Windows itself. However, there are things you can do to ensure that software installation goes as smoothly as possible. Chapter Eight explains how. You'll also learn here how to dual boot (run two operating systems on the same machine). This can be extremely useful in certain circumstances.

There are many ways you can improve the efficiency and speed with which you work. Quick access to frequently used applications is just one and Chapter Nine details a number of useful shortcuts which will save you time and effort.

In Chapter Ten we have placed a number of miscellaneous tips ranging from the frivolous (how to cheat at Freecell & Minesweeper) to more serious stuff such as how to compress individual files and folders.

All in all, there is something for everyone here and the author hopes that, for you, there is plenty.

Windows XP System Requirements

Windows XP is a powerful and complex piece of software, much more so than its predecessor, Windows ME.

Each succeeding version introduces new features and technology designed to improve and further the operating system's capabilities. However, this comes at a price – namely the system resources or requirements needed to run it. This is particularly so with XP.

Therefore, before you get into trying to improve XP's default performance levels, you need to ensure that your system is capable of even supporting those default levels in the first place.

Microsoft's recommended system requirements are:

- Processor speed of 300 MHz

- 128 MB of RAM

- 1.5 GB available hard disk space

- SuperVGA (800 x 600) resolution video adaptor and monitor

The minimum requirements are:

- Processor speed of 233 MHz

- 64MB of RAM

If you try running XP with these minimum requirements or lower you will find that its performance levels will be severely impaired.

The most important of these requirements is RAM (memory). RAM at the moment is cheap and is also very easy to install, so if your PC is lacking in this department get some more if you want to get the best out of XP – 256 MB is not excessive.

Processors are a slightly different kettle of fish as upgrading these often necessitates a motherboard upgrade as well. However, in order to justify the cost of XP, this may be necessary.

To sum up, XP will not perform in a low specification machine, just as a Formula One engine wouldn't if fitted in a Model-T Ford. It needs suitable hardware to support it.

If, after installing XP, you discover it doesn't perform as well as you expected in terms of speed, take a look at how much memory your system has. If it's lower than 128Mb then this will almost certainly be the reason. Contact the manufacturer of your PC and ask exactly what type of memory module is installed in the PC. Then, armed with this information, take a trip to your nearest computer hardware store and buy some more. Then all you have to do is open up the case and plug it in.

Alternatively, disconnect all the peripherals such as monitor, keyboard and printer etc. and take the case into the store with you. They will almost certainly install the new memory for you on the spot.

Startup Programs

On running a new system for the first time, the first thing that will strike an experienced user is how quickly the Windows desktop appears on-screen.

Unfortunately, over time, this will gradually take longer and longer. This process, however, will not be obviously noticeable to the user as it occurs so slowly. The day will come though when it suddenly hits you just how slow the PC's startup has become. There are various reasons for this, which we will cover in the next few pages. Generally, however, the problem is the result of simply using the PC, the act of which will inevitably alter the ideal setup of any new computer.

When a computer is brand new, it will be loaded with a minimal quantity of programs. However, as the user installs more and more programs, some of them will inevitably, either by design or default, find their way to the Startup folder. Programs in this folder start automatically with Windows so that when the desktop appears, they are up and running and ready for use. This can be extremely useful if you use a particular program regularly, a word processor for example.

The downside, however, is that the more programs you have in the Startup folder, the longer Windows will take to load.

The solution to the problem therefore, is to remove as many of these programs as possible. Do this as follows:

1 Go to Start, All Programs and then Startup. This reveals the contents of the Startup folder without actually opening it

2 This menu indicates which programs will start automatically with Windows

Another way of discovering which programs are in the Startup folder is via System Information. This is accessible from Start, All Programs, Accessories, System Tools.

You will also find a lot of other information about your system here.

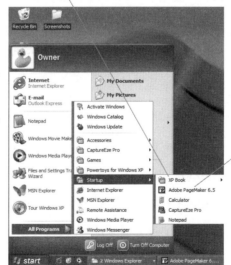

3 Remove any unnecessary entries by right-clicking and then clicking Delete

The more programs you remove from the Startup folder, the quicker Windows will load.

Streamline Your Fonts Folder

Windows XP comes with approximately 260 fonts which are installed in the Fonts folder. This folder can be accessed by going to My Computer, Control Panel, Fonts.

All the fonts installed on your system are listed in this folder

If you do decide to delete any fonts from the Fonts folder, be sure you do not remove any of the Windows default fonts.

Every time your computer is booted, all these fonts have to be loaded into the system's memory along with other Windows applications. The more fonts, the longer Windows will take to load.

The vast majority of these fonts are never used and thus serve only to reduce system performance. It makes sense therefore to go through the Fonts folder and delete all inessential fonts. Keep only the ones you are likely to use and those required by Windows itself. Windows' default fonts can be identified by the date stamp (simply right-click the file and then click Properties). These dates will be the same as the other Windows system files. These are:

As an alternative to simply deleting the fonts you don't use, you could save them to a different folder. This gives you the option of reinstalling them, should you need to.
You could also make use of XP's file compression utility to reduce folder size.

- Windows 95 (retail/SP1) — 7/11/95

- Windows 95 OEM Service Release 2 — 8/24/96

- Windows 95 OEM Service Release 2.1 — 8/24/96–8/27/97

- Windows 95 OEM Service Release 2.5 — 8/24/96–11/18/97

- Windows 98 (original) — 5/11/98

- Windows 98 Second Edition — 4/23/99

- Windows Millennium Edition — 6/8/2000

- Windows XP — 8/23/2001

Screensavers and Wallpaper

Back in the "dark ages", computer monitors were prone to having an impression literally burnt into the screen by prolonged exposure to a static image. To guard against this unfortunate tendency, screensavers were invented. Quite apart from serving a useful purpose, they can also be fun.

These days, however, that's all they are – fun. They are now actually completely superfluous in the modern computer system as present day monitors are not susceptible to damage caused by static images.

Screensavers are notorious for causing system crashes. With XP, this won't present a problem due to its inherent stability but it can be a problem on older Windows versions.

Unless you particularly enjoy watching bouncing balls, fish swimming across your desktop and the like, all you are doing by running them on your system is actually slowing it down. The same applies to Wallpaper. These are actually quite large bitmap image files that have no function other than to make your desktop look pretty. Both can slow down the startup procedure considerably.

In general, graphics of any type, be it a movie file or a picture, are one of the slowest loading elements in a computer system. If you have a highly specified machine, this won't matter too much, the PC will be able to handle them. However, if your PC could really do with upgrading, getting rid of as many graphics as you can will give you a significant performance boost.

You can either disable your screensavers by right-clicking the desktop and then clicking Properties, Screen Saver, or get rid of them altogether. Do this by locating your Windows folder on your hard drive, opening it and looking for a folder called "System 32". Inside this folder you will find all the screensavers installed on your system. To help you identify them they are all prefaced by "ss" followed by the name of the screensaver i.e. "sspipes". Simply delete any you don't want.

To find your Wallpaper files, again, locate your Windows folder and scroll down until you find the images, which you will recognize by their names, i.e. Blue Rivets, Black Thatch etc. They can also be identified by their icon which is the same as that for the Windows Picture and Fax Viewer. More wallpaper files can be found in the Windows folder, this time in Web, Wallpaper.

Another way to easily locate your wallpaper files is to set the Folder view in the above mentioned folders to Thumbnails. This will give you an instantly recognizable graphical representation of the files.

Direct Memory Access (DMA)

Direct Memory Access is a capability provided by some computer bus architectures that allows data to be sent directly from an attached device (such as a disk drive) to the memory on the computer's motherboard. The microprocessor is freed from involvement with the data transfer, thus speeding up overall computer operation.

Previous versions of Windows, by default, left DMA disabled. This was because enabling it with certain drives could lead to serious problems. This isn't the case with XP though, which will actually enable DMA by default if appropriate.

However, there have been reports that in some cases, XP is failing to do this and so it is recommended that you make sure by following the steps on this page.

However, not all drives are compatible with DMA and therefore you need to first check your drive's documentation to see if it supports DMA.

If it does, then you can take advantage of DMA by enabling it as follows:

1 Right-click My Computer on your desktop then click Properties. In the dialog, select the Hardware tab. Click Device Manager

2 Click the + sign next to IDE ATA/ATAPI Controllers. Right-click Primary IDE Controller and then click Properties. In the dialog, select the Advanced Settings tab

Primary IDE Channel Properties

General | Advanced Settings | Driver | Resources

Device 0
Device Type: Auto Detection
Transfer Mode: DMA if available
Current Transfer Mode: Ultra DMA Mode 2

Device 1
Device Type: Auto Detection
Transfer Mode: DMA if available
PIO Only
DMA if available
Current Transfer M

OK | Cancel

3 Using the drop down box under Device 1, select DMA if available

4 Click OK

Defragment Your Drives

Fragmentation is a term used to describe the process whereby files saved to a magnetic disk drive have their data split up on different parts of that disk instead of being saved contiguously. When a fragmented file is accessed, the drive's read/write heads have to hunt about to locate all the different parts of the file before they can be reassembled to the original form. The net result of this is that the time taken to access a file can be increased considerably.

To redress this situation Windows supplies a tool call Disk Defragmenter which basically "undoes" the fragmentation and rearranges the data on the disk into the correct order. Access and use Disk Defragmenter as follows:

 XP's version of Disk Defragmenter has a new feature not found on older versions. This works by placing all the files needed for the Startup procedure together on the hard drive. This is one of the ways in which XP is able to achieve a faster bootup time.

1 Go to Start, All Programs, Accessories, System Tools

2 Click the required drive and then Defragment

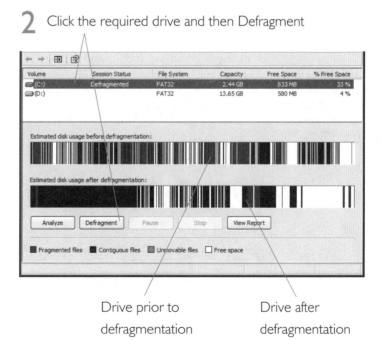

Drive prior to defragmentation

Drive after defragmentation

Disk Defragmenter can also be used on other types of magnetic disk such as Zip disks. It is good practice to run it on your hard drive at least once a month. To make this a bit easier you can set the program to run automatically by using XP's Scheduled Task Wizard which is also accessible from System Tools.

Keep Windows Current

The computer world is a rapidly evolving phenomenon. The technology behind hardware such as disk drives, monitors, motherboards and memory etc. is constantly being revised and improved upon, resulting in a never-ending and expensive battle for the PC user wishing to stay at the cutting edge.

This also applies to the most important part of your computer – the operating system, which in most cases is Windows. Each version of Windows is an incredibly complex piece of software consisting of literally millions of lines of code. Inevitably some of this code will be incorrectly written giving rise to what's known as a bug (error). To correct these errors Microsoft offer free patches (corrections) for download from their website. Quite apart from this however, they also offer various other freebies and system enhancements. Typical examples are the latest versions of Internet Explorer and Direct X drivers. There are also add ons for other Microsoft software such as Word.

As all these goodies, and in some cases essentials, are free for the asking, it makes sense to take advantage. Do it as follows:

A feature of Windows Update is that it can be configured to run automatically. When you are logged on to the Internet, periodically it will activate itself and go off to the Microsoft website and check for any available updates. Should it choose to start downloading one at the same time as you are browsing, it could cause your browser to slow down considerably.

To prevent this you can set it to alert you before it starts downloading. Access the Automatic Updates tab in the System applet in Control Panel.

1 Log on to the Internet

2 Click the Start button and then All Programs

3 Click Windows Update

4 You will now be taken to the Microsoft Update website. Your PC will be analyzed for installed components and then a list of available updates will be offered for download

Windows Performance Options

XP provides a tool which allows the user to easily configure Windows to be biased in terms of application performance over system performance and vice versa.

This can be accessed by going to Start, Control Panel, System. Click the Advanced tab then the Settings button under Performance. Finally click the Advanced tab.

When you open the application you will see that the default setting is in favor of Application performance. The effect of this is that any open program will be given more CPU and RAM resources than any system processes that may be running concurrently. This will get the best out of your programs whatever they may be and is the setting you should generally use.

However, there may be occasions when you need to optimize performance for background services. For example, you could be using the computer as a Web server which would require as much system resources as possible. Windows Performance Options gives you that option.

The default settings for Windows Performance Options will usually be sufficient for the average home user. You will only need to change these settings if you have a resource-hungry application running in the background. Operating the PC as a Web server, as already mentioned, is one such. Another contender is your printer. Printers use a lot of system resources.

1 Set up XP here according to your requirements

2 This option allows you to specify your own Virtual Memory settings

Configure XP's Internal Services

XP configures a number of internal services to start either manually or automatically. As a general rule it does a good job but there will often be times when XP automatically runs services that you don't actually need. The point here is that every running application uses system resources so there are performance gains to be made by disabling any that are not required.

The following services can be turned off without any ill effect:

- *Alerter*
- *Clipbook*
- *Computer Browser*
- *Fast User Switching*
- *Indexing Service*
- *Messenger*
- *Net Logon*
- *NetMeeting Remote Desktop Sharing*
- *Remote Desktop Help Session Manager*
- *Remote Registry*
- *Routing & Remote Access*
- *Server*
- *SSDP Discovery Service*
- *TCP/IP NetBIOS Helper*
- *Telnet*
- *Device Host*
- *Upload Manager*
- *Wireless Zero Configuration*
- *Workstation*

For those of you who find that XP is stretching your PC to its limits, this is of definite interest.

You can access these services by going to Start, Control Panel, Administrative Tools, Computer Management. They appear on the right-hand side of the window as shown below:

Use the tabs as follows:

Description tab	Tells you what a particular service does (assuming you can understand it, that is).
Status tab	Lets you know if a service is running or not.
Startup Type tab	Tells you if the service is configured to start manually or automatically.

Generally, if a service is set to run automatically by default, it is because Windows thinks it will need it. However, Windows isn't always right and if you know for sure that you don't require a particular service, then override Windows and set it to manual. Be aware that this doesn't permanently disable the service, it simply means that it won't run until definitely needed in which case Windows will start it. If it genuinely isn't required however, then it won't run, saving you system resources.

A guide as to how important a service is can be obtained by right-clicking it, which will then open the following window:

4 Click the Dependencies tab

The Dependencies tab is important as it gives you fore-warning of what will happen if you stop a particular service. For this reason it is well worth having a good look at prior to making any changes.

Fast User Switching Compatibility Properties (Local Co... ? ×

General | Log On | Recovery | Dependencies

Service name: FastUserSwitchingCompatibility

Display name: Fast User Switching Compatibility

Description: Provides management for applications that require assistance in a multiple user environment.

Path to executable:
D:\WINDOWS\System32\svchost.exe -k netsvcs

Startup type: Manual

Service status: Stopped

[Start] [Stop] [Pause] [Resume]

You can specify the start parameters that apply when you start the service from here.

Start parameters:

[OK] [Cancel] [Apply]

1 Description of the service

2 Switch to Manual or Automatic start

3 Start or stop the service

5 In the Dependencies dialog box you can see what effect turning a particular service off will have. For example, there may be other system components dependent on it. Alternatively, there may be other components on which the service is itself dependent

Adjust XP's Display Properties

There can't be many computer users these days who aren't aware that they can right-click on an empty area of the desktop, click Properties and under the Appearance tab have access to a whole range of display tweaks.

Windows XP however, gives you even more. Click Start, Control Panel, System, Advanced and Performance Settings. This opens the Visual Effects tab of Performance Options. Here you have a whole range of further options:

Windows in general provides any number of "special effects". XP is even more generous in this respect.

Scrolling menus, fade-out menus, shadows, font smoothing and animation are all examples of these. However, they all consume system resources and the more you have enabled, the less resources you will have available for more important things.

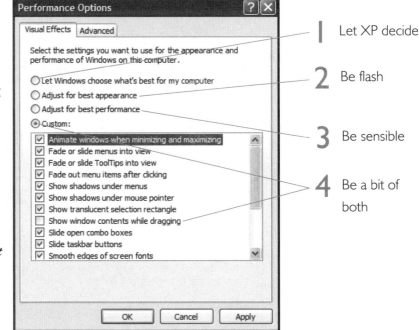

1 Let XP decide

2 Be flash

3 Be sensible

4 Be a bit of both

The more of these display effects you have on, the more the system resources needed to run them. Obviously, if you have a highly specified machine you needn't worry too much, but if you are looking to save resources wherever possible then this is one area where you can make worthwhile performance gains.

Update Your Device Drivers

First, what exactly is a device driver? Well let's assume that you are about to print out a document and have opened your printer software to change a few settings. What you are looking at is actually a driver, in this case your printer driver.

A driver basically has three purposes. Some, like our printer driver example above, act as an interface between the device itself and you, the user, allowing changes to be made to the way the device functions.

Second, all drivers act as an interface between their device and the operating system. They announce to the operating system that they are there and they tell the operating system exactly what they need in terms of system resources to enable them to work.

If you are unable to find a specific XP driver for a particular device, try using one designed for Windows 2000 or NT. The basic architecture of these systems is similar to that of XP, indeed XP is based on them. There is a good chance that your device will work with one of these.

Third, drivers are a way for device manufacturers to update and increase the performance of existing devices. This is particularly important for users of Windows XP.

Many hardware devices currently in use were designed for previous versions of Windows and in the main were compatible with most, if not all, versions.

XP, however, is in many ways radically different from ME, 98 and 95, as many users are now finding out. Many drivers that worked fine with these systems just won't do so with XP. Furthermore, even those that do are in many cases slowing down overall system performance due to their lack of compatibility.

Because of this XP alerts users in two ways if it detects they are trying to use a driver that is possibly incompatible:

- The first comes during the installation procedure and the user may see a message advising that certain devices on their system may not work properly with XP

- The second method is a warning message that will pop up if the user attempts to install a driver that hasn't been approved by Microsoft for use with XP as shown on the next page

Hardware Installation

⚠ The software you are installing for this hardware:

Printers

has not passed Windows Logo testing to verify its compatibility with Windows XP. [Tell me why this testing is important.]

Continuing your installation of this software may impair or destabilize the correct operation of your system either immediately or in the future. Microsoft strongly recommends that you stop this installation now and contact the hardware vendor for software that has passed Windows Logo testing.

Continue Anyway   STOP Installation

There is no need to panic if you see this message, it doesn't mean your system will be trashed. Nine times out of ten, the driver will work fine. However, there is a possibility that it might degrade overall system performance, so don't ignore it.

Pay a visit to the manufacturer's website and see if they have an XP version available for download – it's quite likely that they will. That said, there are manufacturers who have yet to produce updated drivers for Windows ME, never mind XP. You may find that you need to exercise some patience on this matter. Revisit the site from time to time and sooner or later you should find what you're after.

System Restore

System Restore is a Windows feature that was introduced in Windows ME and has been continued with XP.

The application works by taking "snapshots" of the system's configuration and settings at periodic intervals which can be default or user specified. In the event of something going wrong with the computer, you can restore your PC back to a date when it was known to be OK, thus eliminating the problem.

This is all fine as System Restore in fact works very well and can be a life saver at times There is however, a drawback – it eats system resources. Not a problem if you've got plenty of resources to start with but for those that haven't, System Restore is a good place to claim some back. Disable it as follows:

Don't disable System Restore unless you really do need to claim some resources back. It is a very good application and one of these days you could well be very glad of it.

It could be argued that as XP is supposed to be such a stable and balanced system, why is it necessary to have something like System Restore at all? The answer to this is that the application is not just there in case of serious system problems. It can also be used to sort out minor niggles that a user might otherwise decide to live with, albeit reluctantly. System Restore allows you to keep your system free of irritations as well as providing a method of recovering from more serious problems.

| 1 | Go to Start, Control Panel, System. Click the System Restore tab

System Properties

General | Computer Name | Hardware | Advanced
System Restore | Automatic Updates | Remote

System Restore can track and reverse harmful changes to your computer.

☐ Turn off System Restore on all drives

Drive settings

To change the status of System Restore or the maximum amount of disk space available to System Restore on a drive, select the drive, and then click Settings.

Available drives:

Drive	Status	
🖴 (D:)	Monitoring	Settings...
🖴 (C:)	Monitoring	

OK | Cancel | Apply

2 Click here to disable System Restore

3 You can also configure System Restore here (if you have more than 1 hard disk/partition)

4 Click OK

Resource-Hungry Programs

Two programs spring to mind here, neither of which are essential to a computer user.

Antivirus Programs

Quite apart from their negative effects on system performance, antivirus programs can also be extremely irritating in the way they often throw up unnecessary and misleading warning messages. They can also be the cause of more problems than they solve.

No doubt some will be horrified to hear antivirus software described as non-essential but in most cases it really is true.

With the unprecedented explosion in Internet traffic it was inevitable that the Internet would become the prime method for transporting viruses, which indeed it has. However, while millions of people use the Internet for email etc., there are still millions who don't use it at all. These last users have a minimal risk of picking up a virus so what do they need antivirus software for?

Even if you do download from the Internet, it still isn't necessary to have antivirus software churning away in the depths of your system and hogging valuable resources, which they do. All that's really necessary is to fire up your antivirus program when a download comes in, run a check and then turn it off again.

Utility Programs

Many of the functions offered by utility programs, Norton Speed Start (Norton's version of Microsoft Disk Defragmenter) being an example, are superior to the tools bundled with Windows.

Utility programs are third party software which offer various functions to a user such as system diagnostics, repair, tuning and maintenance. Probably the best known of these is Norton Utilities which offers all these plus many more. Other examples include First Aid and Nuts & Bolts.

The one thing that all these programs have in common is that they are resource hungry. Many of the functions can be fired up as needed and then turned off when finished with, which isn't too bad. Others however, such as Norton Disk Doctor, which runs permanently in the background monitoring what's going on in a PC, can be a real drain on system resources.

If you decide to make use of this type of software, try to avoid the applications which run in the background and instead make use of those that can be run when needed and then turned off.

"Spring Clean" Your PC

Formatting your hard drive will literally wipe it clean. You will lose all the data it contained.

There comes a time in the life of any well used computer when it will benefit hugely from a good clearout. Over a period of time, as files are saved and deleted, programs installed and uninstalled, the inevitable crashes occur and users do things they shouldn't, a PC will become literally cluttered up with redundant and useless data, long forgotten files and broken shortcuts, etc. Also, essential system or program files may go missing or become corrupted leading to all manner of niggling little faults and problems.

There is absolutely nothing that can be done about this, it is as inevitable as a politician reneging on his election promises.

So what's the answer? In short, scrap the lot and start again from scratch. This doesn't mean throwing away the computer and buying a new one, but rather junking all the data that's inside it, i.e. on the hard drive.

When doing a Windows installation, it's always better to install on to a newly formatted drive. In this way you can be sure of an error-free installation.

In the past this whole issue of formatting and "clean" installations has been too intimidating for most users to attempt, involving as it did, Startup disks and DOS prompts.

XP however, has simplified the whole procedure to the extent that anyone can now do it. This is explained in more detail on page 137.

The method of doing this is known as "formatting" and this procedure will purge the hard drive of everything it previously contained. Then, you install a new copy of the operating system and finally install new copies of all your programs. The net result will be a PC that is, to all intents and purposes, "brand new". Instead of chugging and spluttering along, it will now roar, much as an old car will if fitted with a new engine.

To do it follow the procedure described on page 137.

Before you do however, you should make backups of all your data and settings. Things to include here are your email messages, email address book, Favorites, passwords and important data such as documents and graphics.

To assist in making your backups, XP provides you with two methods – the File and Settings Transfer Wizard (described on page 147) and its Backup program (see page 177).

At the end of it all your PC will be like a brand new machine.

Use Task Manager For a Faster PC

Common scenario 1

You have several applications running, all of which are essential to the task at hand. However, the PC is struggling to cope with them all and as a result is performing sluggishly. You need to find out which of the applications is using the most memory so that you can close it/them down.

Task Manager can also be used to improve the performance of individual programs by assigning them more system resources.

To do it select your application in the Processes tab, right-click it and select "Set Priority". A High setting will speed up the program. You can achieve the same effect by assigning lower priorities to less essential applications.

A word of warning though. If you're not sure of what you're doing here, it's best to leave well alone.

Common scenario 2

The PC is sluggish and you just don't know why. Something is hogging all your memory but what is it?

The solution to both lies with XP's new improved Task Manager.

1 Open Task Manager by pressing Ctrl+Alt+Del on the keyboard

2 Click the Processes tab

Windows Task Manager

File   Options   View   Shut Down   Help

Applications | Processes | Performance | Networking | Users

Image Name	User Name	CPU	Mem Usage
taskmgr.exe	Stu	03	8,616 K
mmc.exe	Stu	00	1,356 K
mmc.exe	Stu	00	1,352 K
PM65.EXE	Stu	00	5,548 K
msimn.exe	Stu	00	576 K
Winword.exe	Stu	00	456 K
wpabaln.exe	Jenny	00	192 K
OSA.EXE	Jenny	00	44 K
msmsgs.exe	Jenny	00	32 K
CTFMON.EXE	Jenny	00	32 K
MSHTA.EXE	Stu	00	56 K
mmc.exe	Stu	00	740 K
OSA.EXE	Stu	00	52 K
FINDFAST.EXE	Stu	00	344 K
wpabaln.exe	Junior	00	192 K
msmsgs.exe	Stu	00	44 K
Explorer.EXE	Stu	00	3,068 K
CSRSS.EXE	SYSTEM	00	200 K
WINLOGON.EXE	SYSTEM	00	56 K

☑ Show processes from all users   End Process

Processes: 45   CPU Usage: 5%   Commit Charge: 147620K / 18391

3 You'll see all the current applications. On the right, under Mem Usage, you will be able to see exactly how much memory each application is using

Although it's much less common in XP, programs will still occasionally "freeze" or "lock up". Task Manager provides the solution. Simply highlight the offending application and click End task. It won't always be able to do it immediately so give the program a bit of time.

In the event that it is unable to close the program down, then you have to resort to the Reset or Power Off button.

Task Manager is the place to go when you want to discover how much memory your applications are using.

XP's new improved Task Manager is actually much more worthy of the name than its predecessors. Apart from the applications already mentioned, it will also let you open and close programs, switch between running programs, monitor CPU usage and log off.

The Task Manager's Applications tab will show you the main applications currently in operation as shown below:

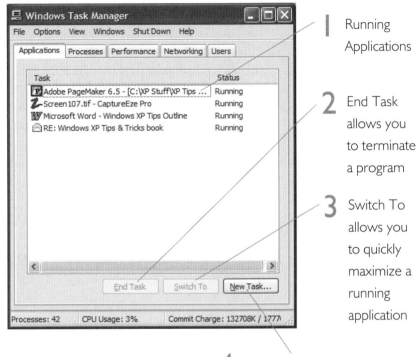

1 Running Applications

2 End Task allows you to terminate a program

3 Switch To allows you to quickly maximize a running application

4 New Task enables you to open a new program

Task Manager also retains its more well known function which is to enable a user to identify and close down programs which are malfunctioning. Programs with a problem will usually be highlighted with the message: "This application is not responding".

Closing a faulty application down with Task Manager is always a better option than just hitting the Reset or Power Off button which can often lead to further problems.

Shutdown XP Fast

While XP is certainly no slouch in the speed stakes it does, like previous versions, have a tendency to drag its heels when it comes to shutting down.

The reason for this is that the system has to close down all the services running in the background. Unfortunately, they don't always close down as quickly as they should. To give them time to do so XP is configured to wait a specified period before shutting down. The amount of time given is set in the registry and by modifying it XP can be forced to shutdown more quickly. This is done as follows:

1   Open the registry editor by typing "regedit" in the Run box.

2   Find the following key:
HKEY_LOCAL_MACHINE/SYSTEM/CurrentControlSet/Control

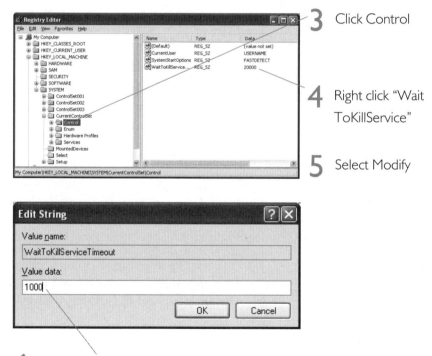

3   Click Control

4   Right click "Wait ToKillService"

5   Select Modify

6   In the Value data box enter a lower number such as 1000

Now you will find that XP shuts down much quicker.

Kill Your Applications Instantly

This may sound somewhat drastic but it can be extremely irritating when certain applications insist on taking their time to close down. When this happens a dialog box will appear prompting the user to either end it now or to wait.

However, by enabling a registry value called AutoEndTasks, non-responding applications will be closed without any user intervention. This is known as *Forced Exit*.

This tip can also be implemented for individual users by going to: HKEY_CURRENT_USER\ Control Panel\Desktop.

1 Open the Registry editor (Start, Run, type "regedit" in the box)

2 Navigate to: HKEY_USERS\.DEFAULT\Control Panel\Desktop

3 In the right hand window locate the value AutoEndTasks

4 Right click AutoEndTasks, select Modify and in the Value data box enter "1"

Reboot for the change to take effect.

Speed Up Your Start Menu

XP's Start Menu isn't exactly slow but can nevertheless be speeded up considerably. This is done via the registry by following the steps outlined below:

1 Open the Registry (Start, Run and type "regedit" in the box)

2 Find the following key: HKEY_CURRENT_USER\Control Panel\Desktop. Click Desktop and locate MenuShowDelay in the right hand window as shown below.

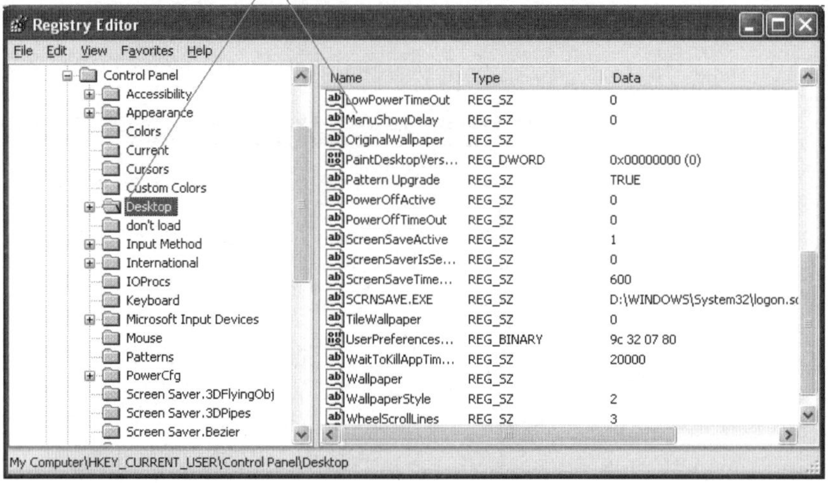

3 Right click MenuShowDelay, select Modify and in the Value data box enter any number between 0 and 400.

400 is the default setting so if you choose any number below this you increase the speed of the Start Menu.

Experiment a bit here. If you choose a low number you may find it's a bit too fast for your liking.

Refresh Rates and XP

A monitor's refresh rate is the number of times a second a picture is drawn on screen by the graphics card. The higher the refresh rate the less noticeable the effect is and perhaps more importantly, the less strain is placed on the user's eyes.

With Windows 98 and ME, users didn't have to bother about the refresh rate as it was automatically set to the highest rate possible. This was known as the *Optimal* setting and was selected by default.

A common misconception is that it is not good for a monitor to run at high refresh rates. This is most definitely a myth. It is quite safe to choose the highest rate available as long as the monitor can support it.

XP, however, will select a refresh rate of 75 or even 60 regardless of the fact that higher rates are available. For occasional users this might not be too much of a problem but when a computer is used for long stretches at a time, it most definitely is, leading as it does to eye strain and even headaches.

So, when running XP for the first time, one of the first things the user needs to do is set the refresh rate to the highest possible level. This is done as described below:

1 Go to Control Panel, Display. Click the Settings tab

2 Click the Advanced button and then click the Monitor tab

However, running a monitor at a refresh rate that it cannot support can cause damage. For this reason always make sure the "Hide modes that this monitor cannot support" box is checked before making alterations.

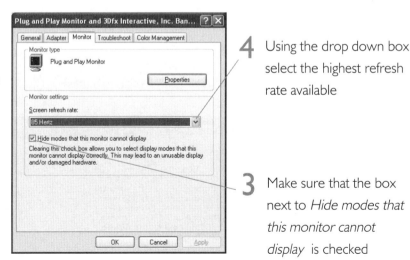

4 Using the drop down box select the highest refresh rate available

3 Make sure that the box next to *Hide modes that this monitor cannot display* is checked

Once this has been done you can forget about refresh rates. XP will now always run with the rate selected.

640 x 480 Resolution

With previous Windows versions it was possible to set a display resolution of 640 x 480 from the settings tab in Display Properties (Start, Control Panel, Display). This setting is commonly used with 14-inch monitors and perhaps because monitors of this size have largely been superceded by 17-inch monitors, Microsoft have seen fit to remove this option as shown below:

1 The lowest setting XP allows is 800 x 600. This is fine if you are using a 17-inch monitor but if you are using a 14-inch model as many still are, you may wish to have this option back

2 Open Display Properties and click Settings. Click Advanced and then Adaptor

3 Click the List All Modes button

4 Now you can set your monitor at 640 x 480

Cosmetic Customization

Windows is a tweaker's paradise allowing all manner of changes to its default settings. This chapter shows just a few of the ways you can change the way XP looks.

Covers

Chapter Two

Restore Familiar Desktop Icons

On running XP for the first time many people are surprised to see that with the exception of the Recycle Bin, all the usual desktop icons have disappeared. Get them back as follows:

1 Right-click the Desktop and select Properties

Using the tip on this page will only enable you to add My Computer, My Network Places, My Documents and Internet Explorer to the Desktop. However, you can add the icons of most applications to the Desktop simply by right-clicking and selecting Send To, Desktop (create shortcut).

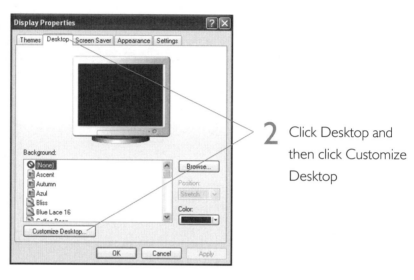

2 Click Desktop and then click Customize Desktop

You can also change the default icons here to something different. You aren't given a great deal of choice though, so if nothing appeals, take a look at page 134 which shows you how to access a greater choice of icons.

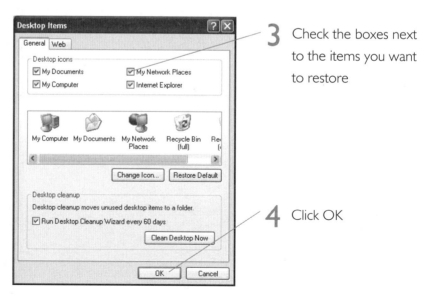

3 Check the boxes next to the items you want to restore

4 Click OK

Configuring XP's Taskbar

As with previous Windows versions you can resize the Taskbar or move it to any edge of the screen. If it won't move, right-click an empty area and uncheck Lock Taskbar.

A new Taskbar feature is the grouping of related applications. Say, for example, that you have three different Notepad documents open at the same time. On the Taskbar you will see "3 Notepad". Click it and you will get a pop-up window showing you the names of the three documents. You can then easily maximize or close them either individually or collectively. The effect of this feature is to keep the Taskbar free of clutter.

Another thing that will be immediately noticeable on running XP for the first time is that the Quick Launch toolbar has disappeared from the Taskbar. This is just one of several changes to the traditional Windows Taskbar.

To get the Quick Launch toolbar back simply right-click on an empty part of the Taskbar and you will see a pop-up menu:

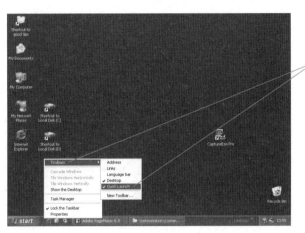

Simply select Toolbars and click Quick Launch

The Links and Desktop toolbars can be restored in the same way as the Quick Launch. Whereas in previous Windows versions the various items would be spread out along the toolbar, in XP you get a single entry which opens a pop-up menu showing every item on the toolbar. This menu can be expanded further to show all links and sub-links to these items.

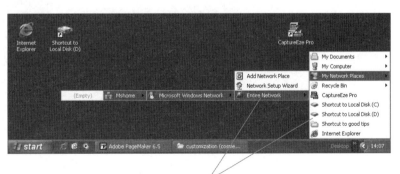

Clicking Desktop reveals a pop-up menu leading to sub-menus

Lose XP's New Look

The most obvious change from previous versions of Windows is the appearance of the Windows XP interface. Gone is the somewhat conservative look of previous Windows and in its place is what some would describe as a scheme bordering on the garish, with chunky and brightly colored buttons.

 The Windows Classic theme removes the XP components from Windows and thus makes it resemble the older versions – to a certain extent. The familiar icons will still be missing from the desktop, the Start menu won't be the same and folders will still appear as Web pages. However, if you are determined enough to find them, there are enough tweaks available to enable you to more or less recreate the old Windows look. For example, you can make folders look like they used to by clicking Tools on the menu bar and then Folder Options... and finally selecting "Use Windows classic folders".

Needless to say many people are not all that keen on it. It would seem that Microsoft anticipated this reaction and so have provided a way to restore the familiar look of Windows.

1 Right-click the Desktop and then click Properties

2 Click the Themes tab

Display Properties ? X

Themes | Desktop | Screen Saver | Appearance | Settings

A theme is a background plus a set of sounds, icons, and other elements to help you personalize your computer with one click.

Theme:

Windows Classic ▼   Save As...   Delete

My Current Theme
Windows Classic
Windows XP
More themes online...
Browse...

Active Window   _ □ X
Normal   Disabled   Selected

Window Text

OK   Cancel   Apply

3 Using the drop-down box simply select Windows Classic and then click OK. After a few seconds the old Windows look will be restored

Changing XP's Icons

As with its interface scheme, XP comes with a set of new-look icons. Again, these aren't to everybody's taste and fortunately it's an easy task to change them to something more to your liking.

To change the icon of a system file or folder such as My Computer or Neighborhood Network, you first have to create a shortcut to the folder. To demonstrate this we will change the icon for My Computer, as follows:

This tip will also work with Windows applications such as Internet Explorer and Outlook Express.

You can also try it with third party programs you have installed yourself. Most of them will give you a choice of icons.

1   Right-click the My Computer icon and select Create Shortcut

2   This will create an identical icon labeled "Shortcut to My Computer"

3   Right-click the shortcut, click Properties and then Change Icon. This will open an icon folder as shown below:

If you really can't find an icon that appeals, you will find literally thousands on the Internet. All you have to do is download them.

It is a good idea to create a specific folder for this purpose. To associate them with a particular application, follow steps 1–3, in step 4 click Browse and find your icon folder. Open it, select the icon and then click OK.

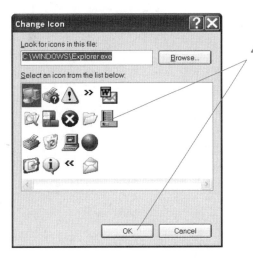

4   Select the icon you want and then click OK. The My Computer icon will now be changed to the icon of your choice

5   Now all you need to do is delete the original My Computer icon. This procedure will work for most system folders. You will also find that many applications will give you different choices of icon

Customizing Folder Icons with XP

This business of putting pictures on icons might seem frivolous to some but it can actually be a very useful method of identifying a folder's contents. For example, you could create text graphics to place on your folders. These could read, Stu's Photo's, Stu's Letters, Stu's Accounts or anything else you want.

Quite apart from changing icons for system folders and standalone applications, XP allows you to change and also customize individual folder icons. This is something that required a third party utility in previous versions of Windows.

Changing Folder Icons

1 Right-click the folder of your choice and then click Properties. In the dialog, select the Customize tab

There is however, a slight drawback here. This is due to the fact that the folder will only display the picture if Thumbnail is selected under Views on the folders menu bar. This means that a folder's picture will not be displayed if it is placed on the desktop.

New Folder Properties

General | Sharing | Customize

What kind of folder do you want?
Use this folder type as a template:

Documents (for any file type)

☐ Also apply this template to all subfolders

Folder pictures

For Thumbnails view, you can put a picture on this folder to remind you of the contents.

Preview:

Choose Picture...

Restore Default

Folder icons

For all views except Thumbnails, you can change the standard "folder" icon to another icon.

Change Icon...

OK | Cancel | Apply

3 To customize the folder by placing a picture on it, click Choose Picture. Browse to your desired picture and double-click it

4 Click OK

2 To simply change the icon click the Change Icon button which will open a window giving you a choice of icon

Create Your Own Icons

Windows comes with a good supply of icons and most people are perfectly happy to use these. However, it is quite a simple task to create and use your own.

You can either design the icon yourself using an image editing program such as Windows Paint or simply convert any image to an icon.

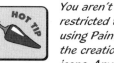
You aren't restricted to using Paint for the creation of icons. Any image editing program will be able to do the same. For example, you can try Paint Shop Pro which is freely available (as shareware) on computer magazine front cover CDs.

Design Your Icon Using Paint

Open Paint by going to Start, All Programs, Accessories and Paint. Click Image on the toolbar and select Attributes.

1 In the Width and Height boxes overwrite the current values by typing 32 in each. This is the standard icon size

Attributes	? X
File last saved: Not Available	OK
Size on disk: Not Available	Cancel
Resolution: 64 x 64 dots per inch	Default
Width: 32 Height: 32	
Units	
○ Inches ○ Cm ● Pixels	
Colors	
○ Black and white ● Colors	

Gridding your workspace will make it possible to create very precise and detailed icons which just wouldn't be possible otherwise.

2 You'll notice that the workspace has now shrunk. Increase it by going to View on the menu bar and then Zoom, Custom. Select the 800% setting

3 Click View, Zoom, Show Grid. This will grid the workspace making it easier to create your icon accurately. Also, click Show Thumbnail. This will enable you to see how your masterpiece will actually look as you are creating it

4 Create your icon using Paint's drawing tools

When you have created your new icon, you must save it as a bitmap. Also, you must "make" it an icon by giving it the icon file extension .ico placed immediately after the name.

Using an existing image to create an icon as described opposite will result in an icon file size of anything up to 1MB. Doing it the "proper" way with an image editing program will result in a file size of roughly 5KB – quite a difference.

However, there is a way around this but to do it you will need a more powerful program than Paint. A good choice would be Paint Shop Pro. With programs of this calibre, there will be features which will enable you to reduce the file size of an icon created from an image.

5 When your icon is finished you need to save it as an icon file. This is done by using the .ico file extension. Click Save As from the File menu, give your icon a name (e.g., House.ico) and save it in a folder. It's a good idea to create an icon folder for this purpose

Creating an icon from an existing image is even easier. Simply open the image in Paint, give it a suitable name followed by the .ico file extension and then save it as a bitmap to your icon folder.

To apply your new icons use the methods described on page 37. The only difference is that you must browse to the folder containing your icons and select them from there.

Get Rid of Those Shortcut Arrows

Injudicious changes to the Registry can have disastrous consequences. Therefore, before you make any changes at all you must make a backup copy in case something goes wrong. This will enable you to "undo" any mistakes.

Go to the File menu and click Export. This will open the Export Registry File dialog box. In the File Name box enter a suitably descriptive name (such as My Registry Backup) and then click Save. By default, the file will be saved in the My Documents folder. You can save it somewhere else if you wish though.

To undo Registry changes, open the Registry Editor and, from the File menu, click Import. Browse to the folder containing your backup and click Open. The Registry will now be restored to its original state.

However, it's possible that your changes will have rendered Windows unusable. In this case reboot and when you see the message Please select the Operating System to Start, press F8. Using the arrow keys select Last Known Good Configuration and then press Enter. This will restore the Registry and repair Windows.

All shortcuts are identified by a little arrow pointing upwards to the icon and many people find them irritating. Fortunately, there is a way to get rid of them. This involves using the Registry, which can be a dangerous place for the uninitiated, so if you decide to use this tip, follow the instructions exactly.

1 Fire up the Registry. Go to Start, Run and in the box type "regedit". Click OK.

2 Click Edit and then Find

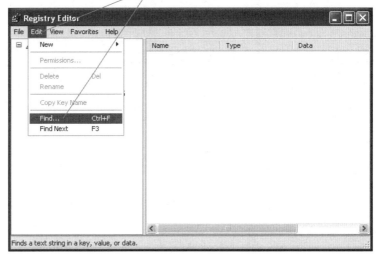

3 Type "IsShortcut" as shown below, then Find Next

4 IsShortcut is the Registry entry which refers to the shortcut arrows. We have to find all instances and delete them. When the Registry finds an instance you will see the following:

Having removed the shortcut arrows you might also like to get rid of the prefix "Shortcut to..." which precedes all shortcuts. This will make your shortcuts appear as normal icons.

All you have to do is right-click the shortcut and then rename it, e.g. "Shortcut to Drive C" could be renamed "Drive C".

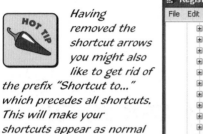

5 Delete IsShortcut by right-clicking and clicking Delete

6 Go back to the Find box and repeat the search, deleting the next instance of IsShortcut. Keep doing this until you get a message saying "Finished searching through the Registry". You will find that in XP Home Edition there are six IsShortcut entries in the Registry

7 Reboot the PC and on restart all those pesky little arrows will have disappeared for good

Create Your Own Wallpaper

XP comes with a reasonably good selection of wallpaper which is stored in the Windows folder. You select them by going to the Desktop tab in the Display Properties dialog box.

However, should you find these uninspiring, it's a simple matter to create your own. All you need is the raw material and XP's graphic editor, Paint (Start, All Programs, Accessories, Paint).

The first thing to do is create your graphic. This can be a photo you have scanned in to the PC or something you have designed yourself with Paint.

As has already been pointed out on page 13, having your desktop elaborately wallpapered can increase XP's loading time.

Once you are happy with it you need to give it the correct dimensions. You can ascertain what these are by right-clicking the Desktop, clicking Properties and then clicking the Settings tab. At the lower left-hand side you will see the screen resolution to which your monitor is set, e.g. 800 x 600 pixels. This is what you need to know. Go back to Paint and click Image, Attributes. This opens the following dialog box:

If you don't like any of XP's wallpapers and you can't be bothered to make your own, the Internet is where you need to go. Here you will find a vast assortment freely available for downloading.

Attributes

File last saved: Not Available
Size on disk: Not Available
Resolution: 64 x 64 dots per inch

Width: 800   Height: 600

Units
○ Inches   ○ Cm   ● Pixels

Colors
○ Black and white   ● Colors

[OK] [Cancel] [Default]

Enter dimensions in the Width and Height boxes and click OK

Now go to File, Save As. Give your masterpiece a name and then, in the Save as Type box, select 24-bit Bitmap. Finally in the Save In box at the top, navigate to the Windows folder on your hard drive. Open the folder and then click Save.

The next time you go to the Desktop tab in Display Properties, your wallpaper will be there along with the default wallpapers.

Create Your Own Control Panel

The Control Panel is a very useful and often overlooked section of the operating system. From here you have access to settings for most of the hardware on your PC, Administrative tools and Internet and Network options. It is well worth exploring and you will learn a lot about your PC here.

If there is a particular Control Panel application which you use often, create a desktop shortcut to it and then drag the shortcut to the Taskbar. Now you will have instant access to it.

It does however, contain some applications which will be of no interest to the average user. Power Options and Accessibility Options are two typical examples.

There are others though, such as Internet Options and System, which you might find yourself accessing frequently.

A handy tip is to give yourself easy access to the ones you use most and forget about the rest. Do this as follows:

1. Create a folder on the Desktop and give it a name such as My Control Panel

You can use the tip on this page to create other customized folders as well. For example, if you do a lot of graphics editing you can create a "Graphics Editing" folder on the desktop and place shortcuts to all the programs you use for this purpose, inside it.

2. Go to the Control Panel and create Desktop shortcuts to the applications you want. Just right-click and select Create Shortcut

3. Back at the Desktop, simply drag the shortcuts into your new Control Panel folder. To make it look like the real thing use the tips on pages 41–42 to get rid of the shortcut prefixes and arrows

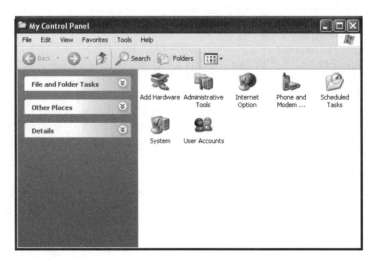

Customize the Start Menu

The Start menu is your gateway to the computer and from here you will have access to every part of the PC.

As shown in the illustration below, it has three main sections:

XP's version of the Start Menu is a considerable departure from pervious versions. While it may not be to everyone's taste, it contains more information and also speeds access to other parts of the PC.

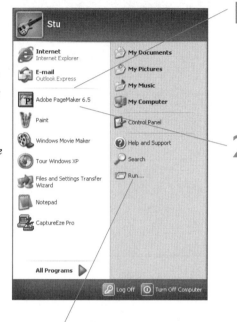

| Items above this line are "Pinned" (permanent). However, they can be removed by right-clicking and selecting Remove

2 Items below the line are the most frequently used programs and the list will update itself automatically. They can be removed in the same way as the "Pinned" items. Right-clicking also gives the option to "Pin" these

Applications on the lower left-hand side of the Start Menu are automatically updated according to frequency of use. You will find that certain (Microsoft) applications seem a little reluctant to make way for others. MSN Explorer is a good example. The author has never once accessed this and yet it remains firmly glued to his Start Menu.

3 Items on the right are placed there by default and you'll find there is no right-click option for deleting these. Do this as follows:

4 Right-click an empty area of the Start Menu and then click Properties

This will open the Taskbar and Start Menu Properties dialog box. Click Customize which takes you to the General tab of the Customize Start Menu dialog:

You can decide for yourself just how many items you want in the Start menu's updated list. This can be anywhere between 0 and 30.

5 Choose the size of the program icons

6 This option allows you to choose how many items are displayed in the list. You can also clear it

You can have cascading menus of the Control Panel, My Computer, My Documents, My Music and My Pictures on the Start menu. This means you don't have to click the item to see what it contains, it is automatically displayed.

7 Clicking the Advanced tab gives you more options:

There are numerous applications such as Run, Help and Support and Favorites, which can be placed on or removed from the Start menu. It's entirely up to you.

8 Turn display of sub-menus on or off

9 Decide which items you want on the Start Menu. There are also options here for how the items are displayed

Adding Items to the Start Menu

Absolutely any item, be it an individual file, folder, program or even an Internet URL, can be placed on the Start Menu where it will then be available for quick access. The way to do it is simplicity itself.

1 Open the folder containing the file to be added

2 Using the mouse just drag it over to the Start button and then release it

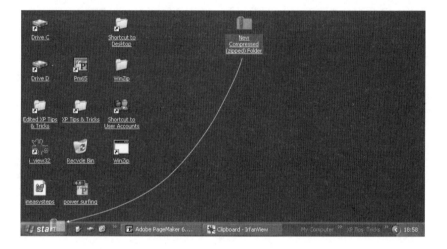

Items added in this way are automatically pinned to the upper left-hand side of the Start menu.

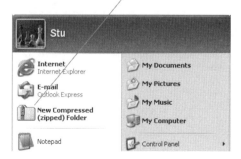

To remove an item, right click and select Remove from this list.

Stop Frequently Used Programs Being Displayed on the Start Menu

A feature new to the Start Menu with XP places the most frequently accessed applications on the lower left-hand side of the menu. This list updates automatically according to the frequency with which individual programs are run. It would appear that this is not of the most popular features of XP and many people would do away with it if they could.

It is of course also possible to simply revert to the classic Windows Start Menu. Click Start, right click and select Properties and on the Start Menu tab check Classic Start Menu.

This is in fact very simple to do and is described below:

1 Right click at the top or bottom of the Start Menu and select Properties. This opens the Taskbar and Start Menu Properties dialog box

2 Click Start Menu and then click Customize

3 Using the Up/Down arrows set the number of programs on the Start Menu to 0

Customize Start Menu	? X

General | Advanced

Select an icon size for programs

⦿ Large icons   ○ Small icons

Programs

The Start menu contains shortcuts to the programs you use most often.
Clearing the list of shortcuts does not delete the programs.

Number of programs on Start menu: 0 ▲▼

[Clear List]

Show on Start menu

☑ Internet: Internet Explorer ▼

☑ E-mail: Outlook Express ▼

[OK] [Cancel]

Now go back to the Start Menu and the Personalized Menu will be no more.

Add Extra Themes to XP

Earlier Windows versions have been somewhat conservative in their default interface look. XP though, takes a more imaginative approach with its chunky and colorful buttons.

Unfortunately, it only comes with three main themes: the default Blue, Olive Green and Silver, so the user isn't given much choice.

However, by firing up your browser and heading off into cyber space, you will discover that there is virtually a limitless amount of themes or *Skins* as they are often called, available for download.

These come in an infinite range of colors and styles and will enable you to make your PC much more interesting visually. The illustrations below show just two examples:

A Skin is a piece of software just like anything else written for a computer and if it has been badly written, i.e. contains bugs, it can affect the way Windows performs. This also applies to anything else you may install on your PC. If an installed Skin does cause you problems then simply delete it.

Many themes come with matching Wallpaper and icons

A good source of XP compatible themes can be found at
www.wincustomize.com. Here you will find thousands of
categorized themes all available for free download.

One thing to note however, with themes downloaded from this
site, is that they require a program called WindowBlinds to be
installed before they can be used. This is a 3.5Mb download and
can be done from the same site. Follow the steps below:

1 First, download your themes by right clicking and choosing Save As.
Then browse to the folder in which you wish to save them and
click Save

2 Now install WindowBlinds and then right click the Desktop and
select Properties to open Display Properties. Click Appearance

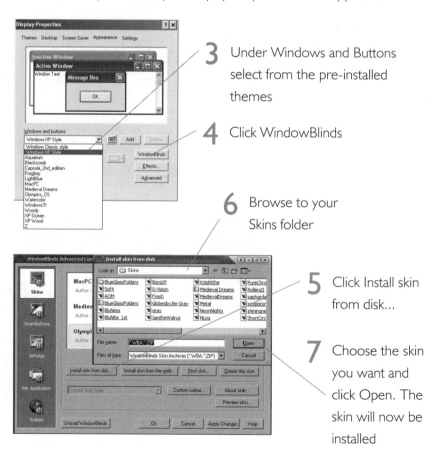

3 Under Windows and Buttons
select from the pre-installed
themes

4 Click WindowBlinds

6 Browse to your
Skins folder

5 Click Install skin
from disk...

7 Choose the skin
you want and
click Open. The
skin will now be
installed

Create a Personal Screensaver

This is a simple tip which is very easy to do. All you need is a supply of pictures. Scanned in photos from a photo album would be ideal. To create the screensaver do the following:

1 Right click the Desktop and select Properties. This opens the Display Properties dialog box. Click the Screensaver tab

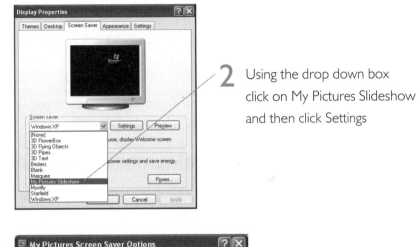

2 Using the drop down box click on My Pictures Slideshow and then click Settings

In the My Pictures Screen Saver Options dialog box you can also configure the way your screensaver runs. For example, you can set the time delay between pictures, the size of the displayed picture and add transition effects.

3 In the My Pictures Screen Saver Options dialog box, click Browse. Locate the folder containing your pictures, highlight it and then click OK

Where's the Clipboard?

Users new to XP may be wondering what happened to the Clipboard, available from Programs with earlier versions of Windows. If you look in XP's Program list you won't find it.

However, it still exists in XP, though for some reason Microsoft have seen fit to hide it away. Now going under the name of the Clipbook Viewer it still nevertheless does much the same things. You can find it as described below:

1 Open the Windows folder on your hard drive and then locate a folder called System32

2 Open the System32 folder and then scroll down until you find a file named clipbrd. This is the Clipbook Viewer

You can also create a shortcut to the desktop as follows:

1. Right-click your desktop, point to New, and then click Shortcut.

2. In the location field, type C:WINDOWS\system 32\clipbrd.exe.

3. Click Next to give it a name, then click Finish and you're all set.

3 All you have to do now is to copy it to the location of your choice. You could for example, pin it to the Start Menu by dragging it to the Start button and then releasing it. Or you could right click and choose "Send to Desktop as shortcut"

Put Your Icons in Order

XP allows you to specify how your icons are displayed in a window. These can be arranged in related groups with headings determined by the type of folder in use. They are usually by Name (alphabetical order), by Type, by Size and by Date Modified. This is demonstrated in the following illustration:

The grouping options offered by a folder will vary depending on its content. For example, a folder containing pictures will allow you to specify the date the picture was taken and its dimensions. Folders containing audio files offer options such as album title, duration and artist.

To do it simply right click an empty area of the folder and then choose Arrange Icons By and finally check Show in Groups. Another example is this view of My Computer:

Here we have different options such as file system, free space and size.

Change the Logon Bitmap

XP's logon bitmap is a plain blue screen that shows for a few seconds before the Welcome screen appears. For those of you who like to customize everything possible, this can be changed to anything you want. A photograph of the user is an example. Do it as follows:

For this tip to work you must enter the full path of the bitmap plus its name. If you aren't sure about this simply right click the bitmap file and then click Properties. Next to Location you will see the full path of the file. You can highlight this with your mouse, right click and select Copy. Then in the Edit String box (Step 3) just click Paste. You will then need to follow this with a backslash and then type the name of the file.

1 Fire up the registry editor (Start, Run, Regedit)

2 Navigate to HKEY_USERS\.DEFAULT\Control Panel\Desktop

You also have an option to tile the bitmap if you so desire. You can do this in the registry editor by right clicking TileWallpaper, clicking Modify and in the Edit String box typing 1. Then restart.

3 Scroll down to the entry called Wallpaper, right click and click Modify. In the Edit String dialog box enter the full path and name of the bitmap you wish to use

4 Close the registry editor, restart Windows and your chosen bitmap will now flash up for a few seconds before the Welcome screen appears.

Display a Logon Message

Many people might find it useful to have the ability to display a message that greets users when they logon. This could simply be something friendly and welcoming or a warning of some description. An example of the latter could occur in an office environment where it is common for company email and Internet facilities to be misused. To create a message follow the steps below:

1 Open the registry editor by typing "regedit" in the Run box available from the Start menu

2 Navigate your way to the following registry key: HKEY_LOCAL_MACHINE\SOFTWARE\Microsoft\Windows NT\CurrentVersion\Winlogon, as shown below

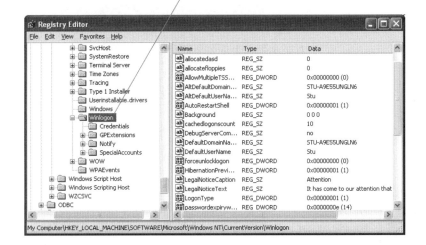

3 In the right-hand window right click LegalNoticeCaption and then click Modify.

4 In the new dialog box type your caption. In the example below it is *Attention.* Then click OK

Edit String [?][X]

Value name:

LegalNoticeCaption

Value data:

Attention

[OK] [Cancel]

5 Now right click LegalNoticeText and again, click Modify. In the Edit String dialog box now type in your message and click OK

Edit String [?][X]

Value name:

LegalNoticeText

Value data:

It has come to our attention that certain employees are misusing the compa

[OK] [Cancel]

6 Restart Windows and you will see your captioned message at the logon screen as shown below:

Should you ever wish to remove the message simply repeat steps 1 to 5, this time deleting the caption and message.

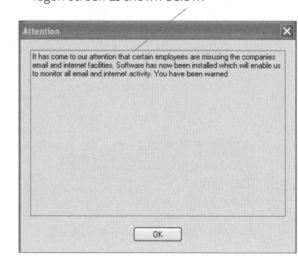

Attention [X]

It has come to our attention that certain employees are misusing the companies email and internet facilities. Software has now been installed which will enable us to monitor all email and internet activity. You have been warned

[OK]

User Picture Icons

For anyone who may be interested, the exact location of XP's user pictures is C:\Documents and Settings\All Users\ Application Data\Microsoft\ User Account Pictures\ Default Pictures.

Each time an account is created, XP assigns it a user picture to help identify the account and also add a bit of visual interest. Many people use picture icons to personalize their account. These pictures will be seen to the left of the account name on the logon screen and on the top left of the Start Menu. XP supplies 23 of these in total. Unless otherwise specified the default picture is one of a guitar. However, it's quite simple to make your own choice as follows:

1 Go to Start, Control panel, User Accounts. Click the account you want to change.

2 In the new dialog box click Change the Picture.

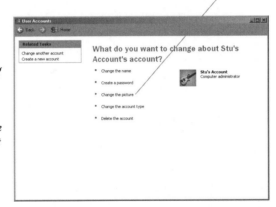

If you are using XP in its Windows Classic theme, you will not see a user picture at the top left of the Start menu. All you see is the account name.

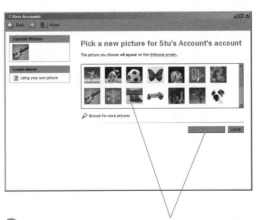

3 Click the picture you want and then click Change Picture

Using Custom Pictures

Not everybody will find XP's list of user pictures to their taste. Many will prefer to use one of their own – a scanned in photograph for example. Alternatively, you may prefer to create one of your own design using an imaging program such as Paint.

Having found your picture, you then need to resize it in an imaging program to 48 x 48 pixels and then click the Save As option from the program's File menu. If you are using Paint you will by default be offered the option of saving to My Pictures which is the folder you want. Other programs will take you to the My Documents folder in which you will find My Pictures. Then click Save.

To use your new picture do the following:

1   Go to Start, Control Panel, User Accounts.

2   Click the account you want and then click Change my picture

3   In the new window click Browse for more pictures

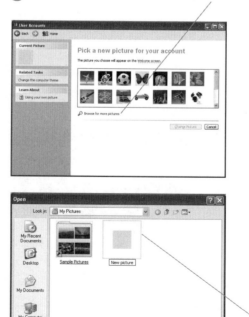

4   The My Pictures folder will now open and you can select the picture you want

System Customization

This chapter demonstrates how changes to default system settings will enable you to enhance your working environment.

Covers

Chapter Three

One-Click Operation

Something that many people are not aware of is that instead of clicking an item twice to open it, there is in fact a way to do it with a single click. To enable this, do the following:

Single-click operation also saves you having to click an item in order to select it. When you place the cursor over an icon it will be automatically selected.

1 Open any folder and from the menu bar select Tools, Folder Options

2 Activate the General tab

While you're at the Folder Options dialog box, take a look at some of the other options on offer. For example if you don't like the drop-down menus on the left side of XP's folders, you can get rid of them by checking Use Windows classic folders under Tasks.

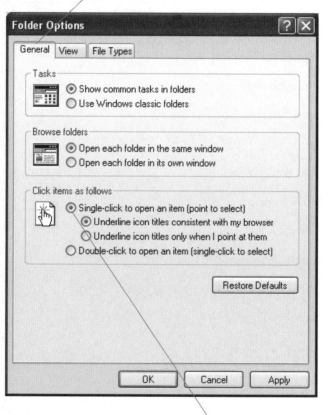

3 Check Single-click to open an item and click OK. Double-clicking will now be a thing of the past

Add Items to the Send To Menu

The Send To menu provides a very useful method of sending a file to an application not usually associated with that file type and simultaneously opening the application. Typical examples are opening a Notepad document in a word processor or a Word document in a webpage editor such as FrontPage 2002.

To do this, all you have to do is right-click on the document, highlight Send To and then click the application. It will then automatically open the document ready for use.

To illustrate how to add an item to the Send To menu, we will add an option for Sending to Microsoft Word. Do it as follows:

As a safety measure, all versions of Windows will by default hide certain folders. In the main these are system folders which contain important data. The average user has no need to access these folders. If they should do so (out of curiosity perhaps) and start meddling about, they can cause damage to their system.

The Send To folder happens to be one of these hidden folders in XP (it wasn't in previous Windows versions). So, before you can add items to it, you first need to "uncover" it as described in step 1.

1 From the menu bar of any open folder, click Tools, Folder Options and View. Here you will see a category called Hidden files and folders. Check Show hidden files and folders

2 Go to Start, All Programs, Microsoft Word. Right-click the icon and select Copy

3 Open your hard drive and go to Documents and Settings. Locate the folder named Owner, open it and find the Send To folder. Simply right click this folder and then click Paste

4 Now right click any document, highlight Send To and you'll have the option of sending it to Word. You can also add other applications in this way

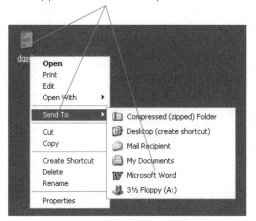

Customize XP's Thumbnail Sizes

In any folder, when you click the View button on the menu bar you are presented with a Thumbnail option. When selected, Windows will display all the files in that folder as thumbnails (miniature pictures). If the file is a graphic then that graphic will be displayed instead of the file's original icon.

You can configure XP to display all your files as mini-graphics or thumbnails.

This feature can be extremely useful in certain applications – a photo album for example. The drawback is that when you open a folder in this mode the thumbnails will appear rather slowly. Also, if the folder contains many files, you will have to do a lot of scrolling to see them all.

The default size of XP's thumbnails is quite large which exacerbates this problem. However, there is a way to reduce them which is as follows:

1 Open the Registry Editor by typing "regedit" in the Run box (Start, Run)

2 By expanding the hierarchical tree on the left-hand side, navigate your way to the following location:

HKEY_LOCAL_MACHINE\SOFTWARE\Microsoft\Windows\ CurrentVersion\Explorer as shown below:

Registry Editor

File Edit View Favorites Help

	Name	Type	Data
WAB	(Default)	REG_SZ	(value
WBEM	IconUnderline	REG_NONE	03 00 (
Windows			
CurrentVersion			
App Management			
App Paths			
Applets			
Control Panel			
Controls Folder			
CSCSettings			
DateTime			
Dynamic Directory			
Explorer			
Advanced			
AppKey			
Associations			
AutoplayHandlers			
BitBucket			
BrowseNewProcess			

My Computer\HKEY_LOCAL_MACHINE\SOFTWARE\Microsoft\Windows\CurrentVersion\Explorer

3 Click the Explorer folder, and then on the right of the window right click and select New Dword Value. You will see a new entry – "New Value #1". Rename this to "Thumbnailsize" (no quotes)

By entering this setting under HKEY_ LOCAL_MACHINE, you are altering the thumbnail size for all users of the computer, assuming you have the PC set up for different user profiles.

To restrict this setting to the current user, i.e. the user making the setting, follow the same procedure only do it under:

HKEY_CURRENT_USER\ Software\Microsoft \Windows\CurrentVersion\ Explorer

4 Right click Thumbnailsize and then select Modify

5 In the new window, type the number 32 in the Value data box. Click OK and close the Registry Editor

Your thumbnails will now be considerably smaller than before. 32 will give you the minimum possible size while 256 gives the maximum. Experiment to find the size which suits you best.

One-Click Shutdown/Restart Icons

To shutdown your computer with XP you need to click Start, Turn Off Computer and then Shutdown – 3 clicks in total. It is possible to do it with one click however, as follows:

1. Right click the Desktop and select New, Shortcut. You will see the following window:

This same tip can also create a Restart icon. Instead of typing "SHUTDOWN -s -t 01", type "SHUTDOWN -r -t 01".

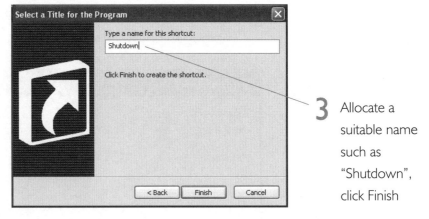

2. In the box type "SHUTDOWN -s -t 01" and click Next

3. Allocate a suitable name such as "Shutdown", click Finish

4. The new icon can either be left on the desktop or dragged to the Taskbar

Changing File Associations

All files are designed to be opened in a specific program or type of program. For example, graphics files such as JPEG and GIF can only be opened by a graphics editing program such as Paint Shop Pro or with a Web browser such as Internet Explorer.

A common problem that many users experience occurs when they install a program on their PC which then associates itself with compatible file types and becomes the default program for opening those files. A good example of this is Paint Shop Pro.

If you find that a newly installed program has hijacked your favorite files, you can send it to the "doghouse" by reassociating the file with your favored program.

Alternatively, you might simply prefer a different application for opening a particular file to the default program.

Whatever the reason, in order to open a specific file type with a program that isn't the default, you need to change its file association. You can do this as described below:

1 Open any folder and from the Tools menu select Folder Options

While in Folder Options you can configure your computer for single-click operation if you haven't already done so.

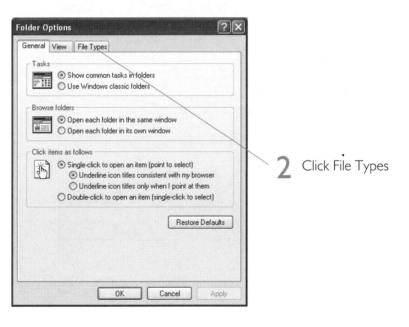

2 Click File Types

The File Types tab lists every registered file type on your computer.

Under most circumstances, the user will not need to make any changes here. However, should the need arise, it is worth knowing your way around file types and associations.

3 Click the file type association you wish to change. In this example we are going to change the program used to open JPEG graphic images. In the Details section we can see that the default program is Windows Picture and Fax Viewer

4 Click Change

5 In the Open With dialog box you will see a list of recommended programs. In this case we will choose Internet Explorer

6 If the program you want to use isn't in the list, then use the Browse button to locate it

7 Using our example, from now on whenever we click (or double-click) a JPEG file it will open with Internet Explorer

Rename the Recycle Bin

XP doesn't allow any options for renaming the Recycle Bin which is silly because many people would call it something else given the opportunity. Examples could be Rubbish Bin, Garbage Can or Get Rid Of.

It can be done however, courtesy of a simple Registry tweak as described below:

As with all registry hacks, make sure you have a good version of the registry backed up just in case things don't go according to plan.

1 Go to Start, All Programs, Accessories, Notepad. In Notepad, type in the following exactly as it is written:

Windows Registry Editor Version 5.00

[HKEY_CLASSES_ROOT\CLSID\{645FF040-5081-101B-9F08-00AA002F954E}\ShellFolder]

"Attributes"=hex:50,01,00,20

"CallForAttributes"=dword:00000000

2 Give this file a name (any name will do) and give it a Registry file extension, i.e. Recyclebin.reg and then save it to the desktop. Click the icon that appears and you will see the following window:

Registry Editor

? Are you sure you want to add the information in D:\DOCUME~1\Stu\Desktop\RECYCL~1.REG to the registry?

[Yes]   [No]

3 Click Yes and from now on every time you right click the Recycle Bin, you will see an option called Rename. Click this and you will be able to call it what you like

Remove Those Error Reports

Whenever an application suffers from an error, and is closed down by the system or by you, the Microsoft Error Reporting feature will pop up, asking if you want to send a report about the problem to Microsoft.

If you're the one in a million who will actually comply, then read no further. However, if you've no intention of ever doing it, then you'll want to get rid of this irritation as soon as possible.

You can do it as follows:

Go to Start, Control Panel, System. Select the Advanced tab

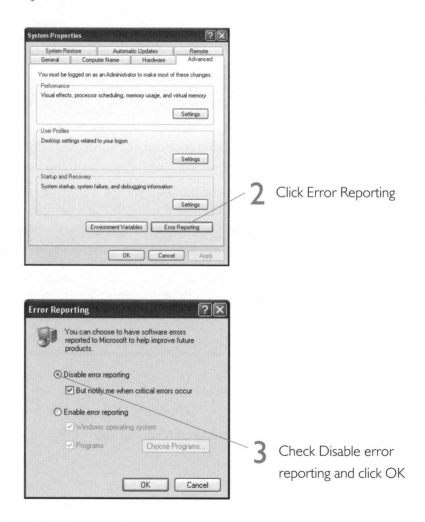

2 Click Error Reporting

3 Check Disable error reporting and click OK

XP Powertoys

Powertoys are a set of handy applications that are available for download from the Microsoft Website. They can also be found on the cover CD of many computer magazines. There are different versions available for the various incarnations of Windows.

The most useful of the applications is undoubtedly TweakUI. This utility enables a user to make all manner of cosmetic and system changes without having to get involved in editing the registry. Its basic interface is shown below:

To download Powertoys aim your browser at: http://www. microsoft.com/ windowsxp/pro/downloads/ powertoys.asp.

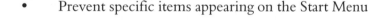

Aspects of the operating system that can be modified by TweakUI

These are just some of the things that TweakUI can do:

All of the Powertoys can be downloaded individually so you don't have to waste time downloading stuff you don't want. They are all about 500KB in size and will take around three minutes to download.

- Prevent specific items appearing on the Start Menu

- Remove or customize shortcut arrows

- Alter thumbnail size and resolution

- Hide drives

- Hide Control Panel applets

- Specify search engines to be used by Internet Explorer

- Hide specified User accounts on the logon screen

- Repair corrupted icons and various system folders

Other Available PowerToys

Open Command Window Here
This PowerToy adds an "Open Command Window Here" context menu option on file system folders, giving you a quick way to open a command window (cmd.exe) pointing at the selected folder.

Alt-Tab Replacement
With this utility, in addition to seeing the icon of the application window you are switching to, you will also see a preview of the page. This helps particularly when multiple sessions of an application are open. To use it you need to press the Alt key and then the Tab key on your keyboard.

Power Calculator
With this calculator you can graph and evaluate functions as well as perform many different types of conversions.

Image Resizer
This PowerToy enables you to resize one or many image files with a right-click.

CD Slide Show Generator
This enables you to view images burned to a CD as a slide show. The Generator works downlevel on Windows 9x machines as well.

Virtual Desktop Manager
Manage up to four desktops from the Windows taskbar.

Taskbar Magnifier
A PowerToy to magnify part of the screen from the taskbar.

HTML Slide Show Wizard
This wizard helps you create a HTML slide show of your digital pictures, ready to place on your Website.

Webcam Timershot
This PowerToy lets you take pictures at specified time intervals from a Webcam connected to your computer and save them to a designated location.

Banish Newly Installed Program Messages

This message has a habit of popping up just as you are trying to access the All Programs, Log Off or Turn off Computer buttons and can be extremely annoying as it gets in the way.

Fortunately, there is a way to prevent it as follows:

1 Open the Start Menu and right click at the top or bottom. Then select Properties

2 This opens the Taskbar and Start Menu Properties dialog box. On the Start Menu tab click Customize and then in the Customize Start Menu dialog box click on the Advanced tab.

3 Now remove the check mark from the Highlight newly installed programs box

Remove the Unread Email Message At Logon

When XP is started it will indicate at the logon screen if any of the named users have any unread emails in their Inbox. For any number of reasons some people might not wish other users of the computer to know this. Turn the feature off as follows:

1 Open the registry editor by typing "regedit" in the Run box in the Start Menu

2 Find the following key:

HKEY_CURRENT_USER\Software\Microsoft\Windows\Current Version\Unreadmail

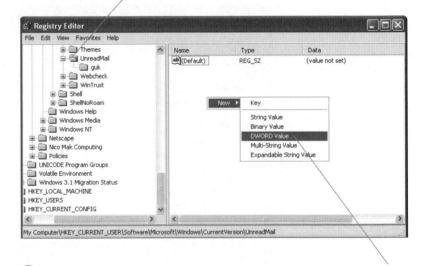

3 Right click an empty space in the right-hand window and select New, DWORD Value

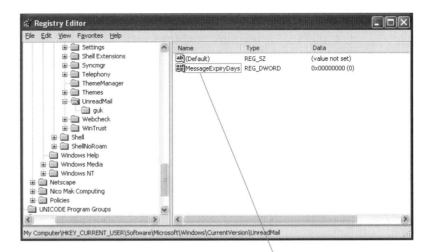

4 Name the new DWORD value "MessageExpiryDays"

5 Right click the new entry, choose Modify and in the Edit DWORD Value dialog box enter "0" in the Value data box as shown below:

Restart Windows and now you will find that the email notification message has disappeared. Should you ever wish to have the message back then simply delete the DWORD Value you created.

Puncture Those Balloon Tips

XP has an extremely irritating habit of throwing up balloon tips which give the user various types of information. Much of this is obvious or will already be known to the user.

For those of you who can do without these tips, the solution is as follows:

 *If you have downloaded and installed TweakUI as described on page 69 in this chapter, you will find that this utility also allows you to disable Balloon tips.*

| Go to Start and then click Search

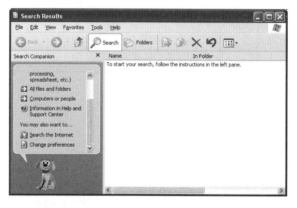

2 Scroll down the **What do you want to search for?** list until you see "Change preferences". Click on it

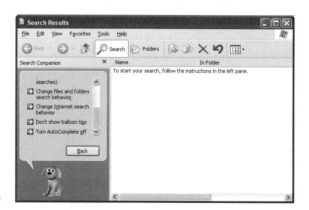

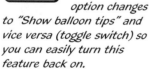 *Once "Don't show balloon tips" is selected, this option changes to "Show balloon tips" and vice versa (toggle switch) so you can easily turn this feature back on.*

3 Scroll down the **How do you want to use Search Companion?** list until you see "Don't show balloon tips". Click on this

Mouse Snapto Feature

This tip will eliminate the need to move your mouse to a certain extent by having the cursor automatically jump to the default button whenever a new window is opened. Set this up as follows:

1 Go to Start, Control Panel and Mouse

2 Click Pointer Options

People with a hand disability which makes it difficult to use a mouse might appreciate this tip.

Mouse Properties ⟨?⟩⟨X⟩

| Buttons | Pointers | Pointer Options | Wheel | Hardware |

Motion

Select a pointer speed:

Slow ——————⊓—————— Fast

☑ Enhance pointer precision

Snap To

☑ Automatically move pointer to the default button in a dialog box

Visibility

☐ Display pointer trails

Short ——————⊓—— Long

☑ Hide pointer while typing

☐ Show location of pointer when I press the CTRL key

[OK] [Cancel] [Apply]

3 Click here to put a check in this box

Try it out. Some people hate it, others swear by it.

Reverse the Mouse Buttons

This is a tip for the "lefties" among you and will enable the button on the right to control primary functions such as selecting and dragging. Do it as follows:

1 Go to Start, Control Panel and Mouse

2 On the Buttons tab you will see an option for reversing the left- and right-hand buttons. Check the box to make the change

Mouse Properties [?][X]

Buttons | Pointers | Pointer Options | Wheel | Hardware

Button configuration

[ ] Switch primary and secondary buttons

Select this check box to make the button on the right the one you use for primary functions such as selecting and dragging.

Double-click speed

Double-click the folder to test your setting. If the folder does not open or close, try using a slower setting.

Speed: Slow —————☐————— Fast

ClickLock

[ ] Turn on ClickLock   Settings...

Enables you to highlight or drag without holding down the mouse button. To set, briefly press the mouse button. To release, click the mouse button again.

OK   Cancel   Apply

Information

The only way to get the best out of your computer is to learn about it and to do that you need information. Windows XP will supply you with everything you need in this respect.

This chapter will show you how to access the various Help applications to be found in XP.

Covers

Chapter Four

XP's System Information

Computers are fiendishly complicated machines and the average user will never get to grips with them completely. However, the more you use them, the more you will learn about them. Some people, of course, don't particularly want to, having no interest in what goes on "under the bonnet" as long as it works.

For those that do though, Windows provides a whole plethora of useful information under various guises.

The first is MSINFO32, also known as System Information.

System Information also provides a useful search engine which can be used to find all instances of a particular word or phrase.

This application can be accessed by going to Start, All Programs, Accessories, System Tools and System Information. You can also open it by typing "MSINFO32" in the Run box available from the Start menu.

When you open it you will see the following:

Under Tools on the menu bar, you will have access to several troubleshooting and maintenance tools. Net Diagnostics, for example, will check your current Internet and email configurations and report any problems it finds.

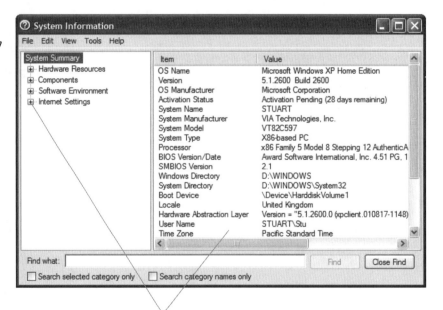

On the left is a hierarchical tree which can be expanded to reveal branches within that tree. On the right you will see related information for each branch

System Information will give you the lowdown on your hardware devices in terms of manufacturer, model number, etc. This can be useful should you ever need to contact the manufacturer of a particular device.

System Information can also tell you which devices, if any, in your system are not working properly. Not only that, it will tell you what the problem is.

System Information also makes a retrievable log of any software and hardware changes made to your system. This can be extremely useful when it comes to troubleshooting.

As shown in the illustration on the previous page the top level categories are Hardware Resources, Components, Software Environment and Internet Settings.

By exploring the various sub-categories you can discover a wealth of information about your system that can be useful in more ways than one.

As an example, let's say you have a problem with your modem and want to contact the manufacturer for some advice. Before you do this, though, you'll need the model number. Unfortunately, you've lost the documentation. So, what do you do?

The answer is to open up System Information. Using our modem example above, you will find the required information under Components\Modem as shown below:

The modem
name and model

In the same way you can find out similar information about every hardware device on your system plus details regarding their configuration.

XP's Help and Support Center

Windows XP also provides a comprehensive interactive database of information relating to understanding and getting the best out of your system. This is accessible from the Start Menu.

1 Do a keyword search. For example, if you want to find out how to use the Device Manager or learn how it works, simply type "device manager" in the Search box

If you are connected to the Internet when you do a search of the Help and Support Center, a simultaneous search will also be made of the Microsoft Knowledge Base. This will vastly increase (maybe too much so) the list of results.

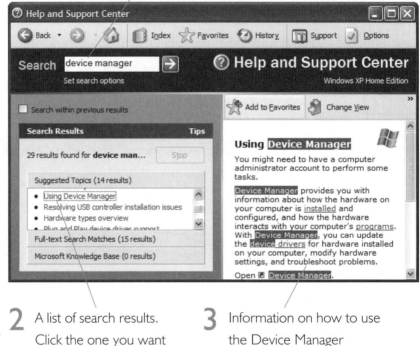

The Help and Support Center is not just about finding answers to problems. It can also be used as a reference source to learn about literally any part of your computer.

So, give Freecell and Solitaire a rest for a while and head off to the Help and Support Center and do something useful!

2 A list of search results. Click the one you want

3 Information on how to use the Device Manager

You also have the option of doing a category search in much the same way you would use a search engine on the Internet. You are presented with a few main topics which when clicked, will lead to further sub-categories. This can be a useful and absorbing way of picking up general information about computers.

XP's Troubleshooters

The troubleshooters provided by XP will take you, step by step, through a detailed and logical procedure for isolating a fault you might have with a hardware device or system process.

Troubleshooting a computer system is not for the faint-hearted. It requires knowledge and a certain amount of courage when it comes to changing configuration settings and so on.

It's probably fair to say that the average user has little real knowledge of what goes on inside that mysterious beige box and so in an effort to help them, XP comes with a comprehensive set of interactive troubleshooters.

Many people, even when they have a problem they are unable to resolve themselves, never even think to consult these troubleshooters, preferring instead to contact computer help lines.

This is a shame because XP's troubleshooters are well designed and written and are extremely detailed. The author, for one, has solved many a problem by consulting them, not to mention picking up useful knowledge at the same time.

Windows XP's troubleshooters include: Printing, Modems, Sound, Games & Multimedia, DVD, Outlook Express and Startup and Shutdown.

You can gain access to them by entering "troubleshooters" in the Search box of Help and Support as detailed on the previous page. Alternatively, you can enter the name of the device or program you need assistance with.

Enter "troubleshooters" in the Search box

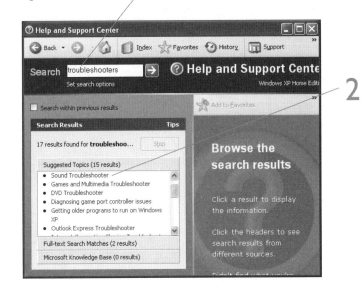

2 A list of trouble-shooters plus other related topics

Microsoft's Online Knowledge Base

If you have an Internet connection then you have access to an enormous resource of information relating to all aspects of computers, the Internet, email and the various versions of Microsoft Windows.

There will be an answer to any query you are likely to have regarding a Microsoft product at this site. You also have the option of contacting Microsoft support staff directly with a question.

Type `http://support.microsoft.com` in your Web browser and you will be taken to the Microsoft Knowledge Base.

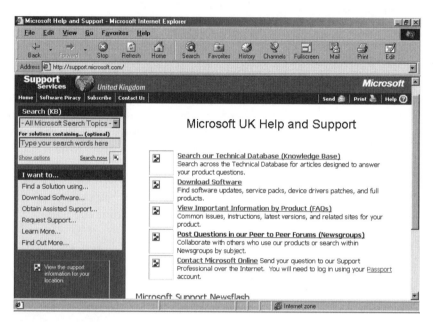

This is a huge and extremely busy site. At times it can be very slow and finding what you want can take a long time.

Here you will find the following:

You can find all manner of device drivers here. There are also links to other driver sites.

Technical Database (Knowledge Base)	A vast list of articles and how-tos providing answers to product queries.
Download Software	Device drivers, service packs, patches and full products.
FAQs	Frequently Asked Questions on common issues, instructions, latest product versions and related sites.
Newsgroups	Swap information and ideas with other like-minded individuals.
Contact Microsoft Online	Send a question to a support professional.

Get More Details About Your Files

This tip is a handy way of obtaining more detailed information about your files. Try the following:

1 Right click anywhere in a folder containing files and then select Customize this folder

The extra columns you select will depend on the type of files in the folder. For example, if they are music files, you can have artist, album title, duration, etc.

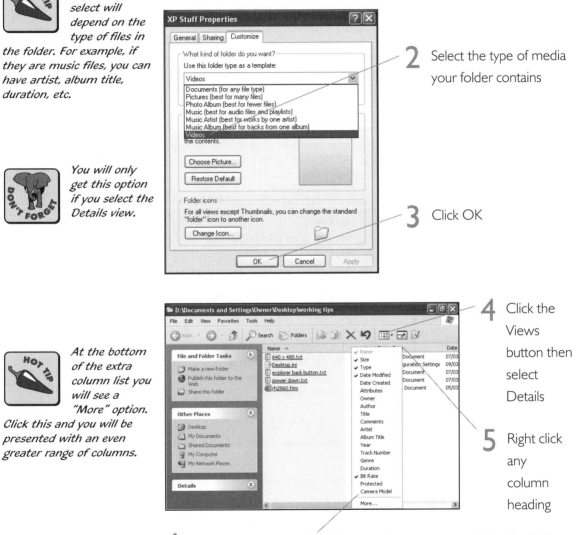

2 Select the type of media your folder contains

You will only get this option if you select the Details view.

3 Click OK

4 Click the Views button then select Details

At the bottom of the extra column list you will see a "More" option. Click this and you will be presented with an even greater range of columns.

5 Right click any column heading

6 Now you will see a list of extra columns you can add to the folder

Device Manager

The Device Manager provides a general view of all the hardware on your system and is accessible by going to Start, Control Panel, System and Hardware.

Using Device Manager, you can see at a glance if there are any problems with your hardware. If so, a faulty device will be identified as such by a colored symbol. You can then investigate that device further via its Properties box.

To get to the Device Manager, go to Start, Control Panel, System and Hardware.

Problem devices are identified by colored symbols.

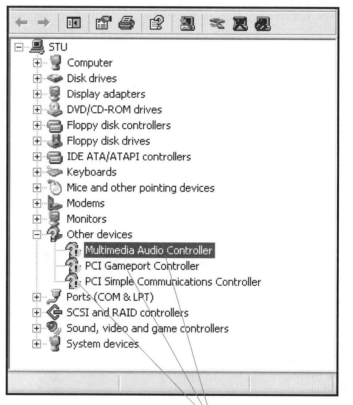

Device Manager tells us that these devices are all faulty. By right clicking a device marked in this way and then selecting Properties, we are given further information about the device as shown on the following page

You can view the resources assigned to your devices by selecting Resources by type from the View menu in the menu bar. This will show you the IRQs, DMAs, I/O and memory currently being used by the system's hardware.

If a device is using the wrong resources (known as a Resource Conflict), you can correct it in the Device Manager.

If you find yourself with a problem you are unable to resolve, you can click the Troubleshooting button, available from the Properties box for all devices. This opens the Help and Support Center with the information you need already displayed.

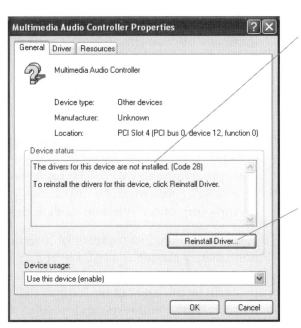

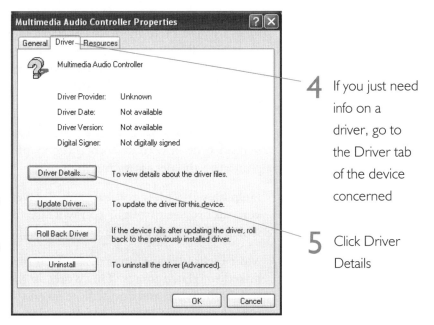

2 Under Device Status, you are told what the problem is. (Here, the driver hasn't been installed)

3 Device Manager allows you to easily reinstall the missing driver

4 If you just need info on a driver, go to the Driver tab of the device concerned

5 Click Driver Details

6 You will now see a list of drivers that the device is using

Read Those Help Files

Good software programs all have one thing in common: they invariably offer an almost bewildering array of functions and features. It's probably fair to say that most people will never use a particular program to its full potential, not because they don't want to but simply because they don't understand how.

Matters aren't helped by some of the terminology associated with various types of application. Graphics editing software is a good example. Explore the various options on the menu bar of one of these programs and you will be regaled by such terms as "grayscale", "dithering", "transparency" and "gamma correction". Gamma correction! What on earth does that mean?

Take a look on your program's installation disks. Here you will often find more Help files and also "Readme" files which will give more recent information about the product.

Faced with these incomprehensible terms, many people are immediately put off and will revert to a more simple and straightforward program of the genre. Unfortunately, by doing this they will be missing out on features that would enable them to achieve a better end result and usually with less effort.

This really isn't necessary – help is almost always just a click away. On the right-hand side of the menu bar on all but the most basic programs is a Help menu leading to a Help file. Obviously, some of these will be better than others, but generally they are well written and explain everything that the program is capable of doing. Many Help files also offer examples of how to use a particular feature.

Microsoft Word has a feature called "Show me" that will actually demonstrate how to do something by physically moving the mouse pointer to the necessary menu options.

Help files also offer an Index which gives a list of keywords that you can browse through. You will also find a Search or Find option which allows you to enter your own keywords.

Most Help files are interactive which means that certain words are linked to related topics. This works in the same way as a web page – click the word and you will be taken to the related subject. If it's not what you are looking for, then click the Back button to return to the original page.

Windows Upgrade Catalog

Because XP is built around the architecture used for Microsoft's premier operating system Windows 2000, it is a radical departure from the earlier versions of Windows.

One of the knock-on effects of this as far as the user is concerned is the issue of hardware and software compatibility. Many products which worked fine with ME, 98 and 95 just will not do so with XP. Therefore, before you go out and buy something, you need to be sure that it is compatible with XP.

One way of doing this is to look for the Designed for Microsoft Windows XP logo on the product packaging as shown below:

Another way is to use the Microsoft XP Upgrade site which you can find at: http://www.microsoft.com/windows/catalog/catalogshell/shell.asp?subid=22.

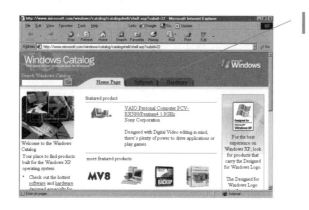

Click Software or Hardware and you will be taken to a list of products which have been passed by Microsoft as suitable for use with XP

NOTE: The list of products is by no means exhaustive. Just because a product is not listed it doesn't mean that it won't work with XP. However, you can be sure that any product that *is* listed will be compatible with XP.

Dr Watson

Dr Watson is a little known diagnostic and information utility that can also be found in previous versions of Windows. While, generally speaking it is of little use to the average user, being intended to gather specific information regarding certain parts of the system for troubleshooting purposes, it can nevertheless be a useful source of information.

This application is primarily intended for troubleshooting purposes. However, you can use it to obtain information about your system.

You can access Dr Watson as follows:

1 Go to Start, Run and in the box type "drwatson". The program will now be minimized to the system tray (on the right of the taskbar where the clock is)

2 Double click the icon and Dr Watson will take a snapshot of the system and then open in its Standard view. From View on the menu bar choose Advanced View

```
[untitled] - Dr. Watson                                    _ □ ×
File   View
 Diagnosis │ System │ Tasks │ Startup │ Hooks │ Kernel Drivers │ User Drivers │ MS-DOS Drivers │ 16-bit Modules │
 ┌─ System ──────────────────────────────────────────────────────────────────┐
 │ Microsoft Windows 98 4.10.1998                                             │
 │ Clean install using CD                                                     │
 │                                                                            │
 │ IE 5 5.00.2314.1003                                                        │
 │ Uptime: 0:14:57:41            Normal mode                                  │
 │ On "STU" as ""                                                             │
 └────────────────────────────────────────────────────────────────────────────┘
 ┌─ Computer ────────────────────────────────────────────────────────────────┐
 │ AuthenticAMD AMD-K6(tm) 3D processor                                       │
 │ 64MB RAM                                                                   │
 └────────────────────────────────────────────────────────────────────────────┘
 ┌─ Resources ───────────────────────────────────────────────────────────────┐
 │ 39% system resources free                                                  │
 │ Windows-managed swap file on drive C (994MB free)                          │
 │ Temporary files on drive C (994MB free)                                    │
 └────────────────────────────────────────────────────────────────────────────┘
 System snapshot taken on 21/10/02 11:51:01.                    ┌─  OK  ─┐
```

3 By clicking the various tabs you will be able to access information on various parts of the system. Dr Watson will also tell you if it finds any problems

Email

One of the biggest problems people experience when using email is that of unsolicited junk mail. These often contain attachments which could themselves contain a virus. This chapter tells you how to eliminate this problem.

There are also tips on how not to lose your email messages and settings, plus some useful shortcuts.

Covers

Chapter Five

Put An End To Junk Mail

Giving out your email address willy-nilly is the surest way of ending up with an Inbox bulging with unsolicited junk mail.

Email is by far the most popular Internet application. It does, however, also give rise to one of the most unpopular spin-offs of the Internet – namely junk email, or "spam", as it's termed.

This section shows you how to banish spam from your Inbox.

Don't give out your email address

Be extremely careful to whom you give your address. Never, ever give it to a newsgroup or chatroom or to websites offering online surveys, prize competitions and the like.

Take the time to learn about cookies. There are any number of websites which will give you the lowdown on this subject.

Cookies

A cookie is a small text file that is downloaded to your PC by websites when you visit them. The cookie enables the site to recognize you and can, for example, obviate the need for you to re-enter your password if you have one. When used responsibly in this way they can be very useful for both parties.

Cookies aren't all bad. Properly used they can be beneficial to both you and the websites you access.

However, certain types of cookie (known as third-party cookies) can be used to extract your email address without your knowledge. Email addresses acquired in this way often end up on lists which are then sold to spammers. You can prevent this as follows:

1 Go to Start, Control Panel, Internet Options. Click the Privacy tab

If you elect to block all cookie use, Internet Explorer will certainly do it for you. However, you will find that as you browse the Net, you will be plagued by constant messages requesting permission for cookie use. You will find it a lot easier just to select a medium setting.

Internet Properties

General | Security | Privacy | Content | Connections | Programs | Advanced

Settings

Move the slider to select a privacy setting for the Internet zone.

Low

- Restricts third-party cookies that do not have a compact privacy policy
- Restricts third-party cookies that use personally identifiable information without your implicit consent

Import... | Advanced... | Default

Web Sites

To override cookie handling for individual Web sites, click the Edit button.

Edit...

OK | Cancel | Apply

2 By moving the slider you can set various security levels for the use of cookies

You can also choose to delete spam from the server, not to download it at all, or to place it in specified folders.

Outlook Express provides another means of blocking email. This is a "Blocked senders" list, also available from the Message Rules dialog box.

This feature allows you to place email addresses on a list which can be upgraded and modified. All emails from these addresses will be automatically placed in the Deleted items folder. This method of blocking emails is particularly suited to messages from unwelcome individuals rather than mass market emails.

The "Friend" message rule will automatically send all emails with "Friend" in the To: box to the Deleted items folder. This one message rule alone will eliminate a large proportion of junk mail. It won't however, eliminate it all, so occasionally you'll have to create a new message rule for spammers who use a different word in the To: box.

Getting rid of spam

However, if you choose to ignore this advice you may well find yourself receiving a dozen or more junk emails every time you log on. Fortunately, Outlook Express provides a way of eliminating junk mail. This is done by setting up filters or message rules.

Before we do this though, we need to find a characteristic common to junk emails. One such will be found in the To: box in the message header of a spam message. Spam generated from lists will be given a "catch-all" address as it isn't practical for the spammer to personalize each address. Typically, this will be the word "Friend".

What we have to do therefore is create a message rule which will block all emails with "Friend" in the message header To: box.

1 In Outlook Express' menu bar, go to Tools, Message Rules and Mail. This opens the New Mail Rule dialog box. Click New

2 Under Conditions, check "Where the To line contains people"

3 In the Actions box, check "Delete it"

4 Under Descriptions, click the "contains people" link

5 In the Select People dialog box, type "Friend"

6 Click Add and then OK

7 Give your new rule a relevant name

Backup/Restore Email Messages

If you wish to change the default folder that Outlook Express uses to store messages, go to Tools, Options, Maintenance. Click Store Folder and you will see the folder currently being used and its location. By clicking the Change button you can specify a different folder and location.

The ability to send and receive email is a very important function of the modern day computer and just as people often like to keep personal letters, they also like to keep their email. Email is also an important means of business communication and these emails need to be kept as records.

Unfortunately, Outlook Express, which is the email program used by most people, does not provide a simple means of creating backup copies of its message folders. There is a way to do it though.

Because your messages are instantly available as soon as you open Outlook Express, this indicates that Windows has a copy of them somewhere. What you have to do is locate this folder and then simply copy its contents to the backup medium of your choice. Do this as described below:

Manual backups created as described on this page will need updating at regular intervals.

1 Open any folder, click Tools, Folder Options and then View. Select the Show hidden files and folders option

2 Create a folder on the drive of your choice and give it a descriptive name such as "My Emails". Do this by simply right clicking, and selecting New, Folder. Then type the name

3 Open your hard drive and go to Documents and Settings, Owner, Local Settings, Application Data, Identities. Then open successive folders until you see one called Outlook Express. This is the folder that contains your emails and you will recognize them by the .DBX file extension

Another, more laborious way to backup your emails is to individually open each message in a separate window by double-clicking it and then, from the Edit menu, select Save As. You can then save it where you like. However, while this will create a separate copy of your messages, you will not be able to restore them to Outlook Express.

4 Open the Outlook Express folder. On the Tool bar select Edit, Select All, Copy

5 Close the window and go back to your newly created My Emails folder. Right click it and select Paste. That's it

6 Should you ever lose the emails in Outlook Express for whatever reason, then reverse the above procedure to restore them

Backup/Restore Email Settings

Backing up your email settings is perhaps not quite so important as backing up your email messages as described on the previous page. After all, the necessary information can always be re-entered if need be. Nevertheless, it can be a bit of a pain to do, particularly if you're unsure of the procedure. This is especially the case if you have several email accounts, as many people do.

Fortunately, Outlook Express does provide an easy way to backup your account settings for restoration purposes in the event of a new installation or disaster of some kind.

When creating backups of data and settings, remember to give the folders a name which will allow you to quickly identify what they contain. Also, remember where you have put them. Floppy disks are an ideal medium for doing this. They can be labeled and put somewhere safe.

1 Create a backup folder with a suitable name – "Email Settings", say. Then, in Outlook Express, go to Tools, Accounts. Click the Mail tab

2 Select the account to be backed up

3 Click Export

4 Open the backup folder and click Save

5 Should you ever need to restore your settings, then simply reverse the above procedure, only this time click Import in the Mail dialog box rather than Export

Backup/Restore Your Address Book

Many people make very good use of their Address Book. Not only can they store all their email addresses in it but also other useful information such as addresses, telephone numbers and personal information.

If they should ever lose all this information which has probably been compiled over a period of years, it could be nothing short of a minor disaster to them.

To guard against this possibility, a backup copy should be made. Fortunately, Outlook Express makes this easy.

1 On Outlook Express' Toolbar, click Addresses. This opens your Address Book

2 From the Address Book menu bar, go to File, Export and then select Address Book (WAB)

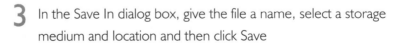

3 In the Save In dialog box, give the file a name, select a storage medium and location and then click Save

4 To restore your Address Book, repeat steps 1 and 2, only this time select Import and then browse to wherever your backup is located and then click Open

Easy Email

This is a handy tip for those of you who do a lot of emailing. Instead of firing up Outlook Express each time you want to send a message to someone and then clicking the Create mail button on the menu bar, you can achieve the same thing from the desktop with one click. Here's how to do it:

1   Right click the Desktop and select New, Shortcut. You will see the following dialog box:

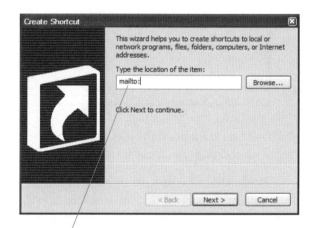

2   In the box type "mailto:" then click Next

3   Type a suitable name and then click Finish

4   You will now see a new Outlook Express icon on your Desktop. Click it and a new email message window will appear

...cont'd

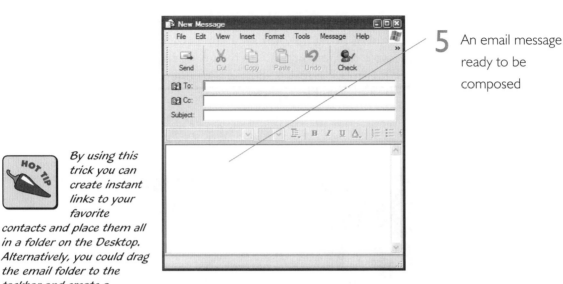

5 An email message
ready to be
composed

By using this trick you can create instant links to your favorite contacts and place them all in a folder on the Desktop. Alternatively, you could drag the email folder to the taskbar and create a pop-up toolbar.

As a refinement of this tip, you can have the message box open with the address already filled in.

To do this all you have to do is enter the required email address immediately after the "mailto:" in step 2. For example if you enter `mailto:stuart.yarnold@ntlworld.com`, your email will open with this address in the To: box.

You can create pre-addressed message boxes to anyone you like simply by entering their email address after "mailto:".

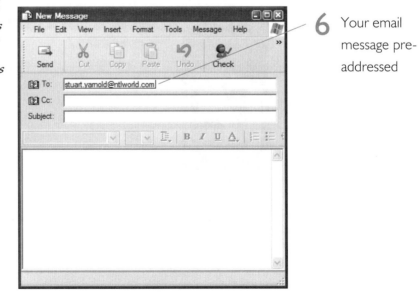

6 Your email
message pre-
addressed

Get Rid Of Email Attachments

Saving unwanted attachments is a pretty pointless exercise. They can often be quite large in size and will simply be a waste of your hard drive space.

Email attachments can be a real pain. For starters, they are all too often frivolous in content and can also be quite large in size, taking up valuable hard drive space. There is also the real risk that a particular attachment may contain a virus. So, if you don't want to keep an attachment or don't want to even open it in case it contains a virus, all you can do is delete the email. The problem with doing this is that you may actually want to keep the email itself – it's just the attachment you don't want.

Unfortunately, Outlook Express doesn't provide any obvious way of deleting an attachment whilst keeping the email it is attached to. It's either all or nothing.

There is, however, a way to do it as follows:

1 Highlight the email and then from the File menu, select Save As

By using the tip on this page you can get rid of an attachment and still have the message available in Outlook Express.

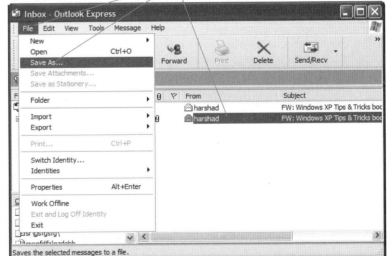

2 In the Save Message As dialog box, do the following:

- In the Save In box, select Desktop
- In the File Name box, enter any name and end it with .eml
- In the Save As type box, select Text Files (*.txt)

This is demonstrated in the illustration on the next page.

3 Now click Save. The file will appear on the Desktop identified by the Outlook Express email envelope icon

4 Delete the original email (and attachment) from Outlook Express by right clicking and choosing Delete

5 Re-size the Outlook Express window so you have access to the new file on the Desktop. Now all you have to do is drag the file back into the Outlook Express window. Open it and you have the message but not the attachment

Basically, how this works is that by saving the message as a text file, you are stripping out the attachment. Giving the file the .eml file extension associates it with Outlook Express. This is what allows you to drag the file back into Outlook Express.

Automatically Re-Size Email Pictures

As most people who regularly use email will know, Outlook Express allows users to either insert images directly into the email or attach them as a file. The commands for these actions are on the Insert menu.

Images attached in this way will be reduced in size by approximately 50%.

The problem with this is that unless the pictures have already been reduced in size in an imaging program, a process of which many people are unsure, you can end up sending an email which will take ages for the recipient to receive. A lot of people find this extremely irritating.

However, once again XP comes to the rescue with it's email image reducing feature. To use it do the following:

| Instead of opening Outlook Express, right click the image you want to send with your email, select Send to and then Mail Recipient.

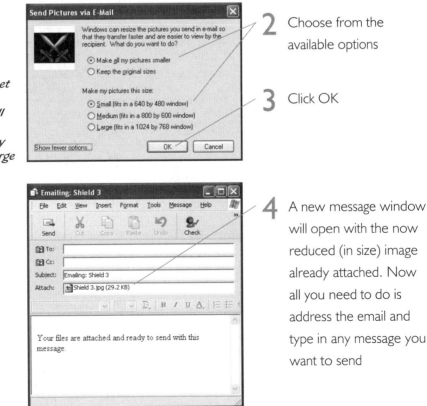

2 Choose from the available options

3 Click OK

Some Internet Service Providers will not accept emails if they are over a certain size. Large image attachments are usually the cause of this.

4 A new message window will open with the now reduced (in size) image already attached. Now all you need to do is address the email and type in any message you want to send

Outlook Express Keyboard Shortcuts

F1	Open help.
CTRL+A	Select all messages.
CTRL+P	Print the selected message.
CTRL+M	Receive and send email.
CTRL+D	Delete.
CTRL+N	Open a new message.
CTRL+SHIFT+B	Open the address book.
CTRL+R	Reply to message author.
CTRL+F	Forward a message.
CTRL+SHIFT+R	Reply to all.
CTRL+I	Go to Inbox.
CTRL+> and CTRL+<	Go to next and previous message in the list.
ALT+ENTER	View properties of a selected message.
F5	Refresh news headers and messages.
CTRL+U and CTRL+SHIFT+U	Go to next unread message and news conversation.
CTRL+Y	Go to a folder.
CTRL+O	Open a selected message.
CTRL+ENTER	Mark a message as read.
CTRL+SHIFT+A	Mark all news messages as read.
CTRL+W	Go to a newsgroup.
LEFT ARROW and RIGHT ARROW	Expand or collapse a news conversation.
CTRL+J	Go to next unread newsgroup.
CTRL+SHIFT+M	Download news for offline reading.
ESC	Close a message.
F3	Find text.
CTRL+SHIFT+F	Find a message.
CTRL+TAB	Switch among Edit, Source and Preview tabs.
CTRL+K and F7	Check names and spelling.
CTRL+SHIFT+S	Insert signature.
CTRL+ENTER	Send a message.

The Internet

There are many tips and tricks to help you get the best out of the Internet. These include increasing the reliability of your connection, increasing your browsing speed and recovering from broken downloads.

Covers

Chapter Six

Minimize Broken Downloads

Download managers can be configured to begin a download at a specified time. They will automatically make the Internet connection using your Dial Up Network settings, begin the download and when it is completed, break the connection. If your connection should fail during the download for some reason, they will redial and then resume the download.

Anyone who downloads data from the Internet will at one time or another experience the frustration of suffering from an unexpected disruption to their download. This can be a result of the modem going offline for some reason or the Internet service provider (ISP) breaking the connection (many ISPs will deliberately sever the connection after a set period).

Murphy's law states that this will happen as the download is nearing completion. You then have to start the process all over again. This is not too bad if it is a small download but if you are downloading a large program you could have wasted several hours.

While there are things you can do to optimize your connection and thus minimize the risk of a broken connection (discussed on page 105–106), there is no way to eliminate this problem completely. However, there is a way to minimize its effects. This comes in the form of what's known as a "download manager".

These are programs which monitor a download and if it is broken for whatever reason, can resume it from the point at which the download stopped. This means you don't have to start again from the beginning. They also offer other useful features such as increased download speeds, automatic scheduling, automatic redial and easy to see details regarding file size, download time, and so on.

There are various programs of this type on the market, two popular ones being GetRight and Gozilla. Both of these are easily obtainable from computer magazine cover CD's. You can also download them from the manufacturers' websites. To download GetRight go to www.getright.com. Gozilla is available at www.gozilla.com.

Both of these programs are shareware applications which means you don't have to pay for them as long as you are prepared to put up with various advertisements and reminders.

The illustration below is taken from GetRight and shows a download in progress. Various information is available from this window.

Download managers can often increase the download speed of a file.
They do this by building a list of "mirror sites", all of which have the file available for download. During the download, the program will automatically switch between the mirror sites to find the one offering the best download conditions.

Download managers such as GetRight and Gozilla are free. However,
this means you will be constantly regaled by a never-ending series of banner ads. The only way to get rid of these is to buy the program outright.

Name of the file being downloaded   Progress indicator   The size of the file

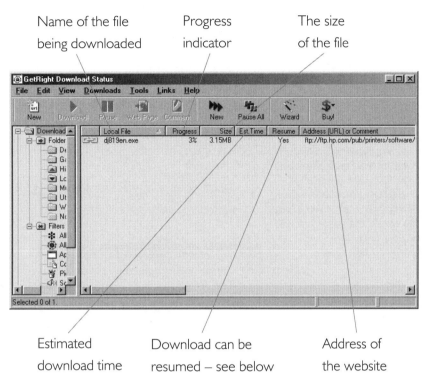

Estimated download time   Download can be resumed – see below   Address of the website

One possible restriction to a download manager's ability to resume an interrupted download is a result of some websites not allowing download resumptions. GetRight checks if this is the case and indicates either Yes or No in the Resume column as shown above.

Change Internet Explorer's Default Start Page

When you fire up Internet Explorer, not surprisingly, it immediately heads for the Microsoft website. It does this because during the XP installation procedure, the Microsoft site is installed as the default Startup Web page. If you seldom or never visit this particular site, it can be a pain. It would be much more practical if Internet Explorer took you straight to a site that you visit frequently. For example, if you use the Internet to keep track of your share prices, as many do, you could go directly to the desired website that you use for this purpose.

A common trick employed by many Internet service providers (ISPs) is to automatically set Internet Explorer's Start Page to their own site when their software is installed. They will replace the existing Start page in so doing. Using the tip on this page you will be able to restore your preferred Start page.

To configure Internet Explorer to do this, do the following:

1 Go to Start, Control Panel, Internet Options. In the dialog box that appears, select the General tab

If you wish to use a specific page within a site as the Start page but aren't sure of what URL to enter, do the following. Simply log on, open the desired page in your browser and in the address bar at the top you will see the page's URL. Make a note of it and then go to Internet Properties and enter it as described opposite.

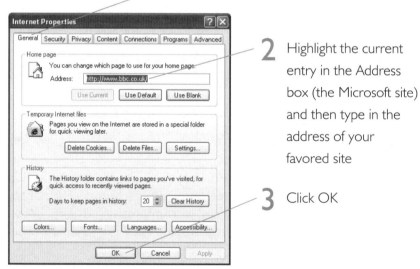

2 Highlight the current entry in the Address box (the Microsoft site) and then type in the address of your favored site

3 Click OK

Using the above example, from now on, each time you start Internet Explorer it will automatically go to the BBC website at www.bbc.co.uk.

Optimize Your Internet Connection

If you are one of the growing number of people now using Broadband for your Internet connections, then this section won't be for you. However, if you are still using a modem and phone line to connect, you will probably be well aware of the sort of problems you get with this type of connection. In a nutshell, these are:

Broadband is a term used to describe a relatively recent type of Internet connection. These connections are typically always "on", so the user never has to log on and off. They also offer data transfer speeds up to 10 times faster than the standard modem/phone line setup. Another advantage of Broadband is that it offers much more reliable connections.

- Arbitrary disconnections

- Slow connections/downloads

Before we go any further it must be made clear that you will never have a really reliable and efficient Internet connection with a telephone line. The reason for this is quite simple – telephone lines were not designed for carrying the vast amount of data that the Internet generates, thus they are inherently unsuitable for this task. The reason they are used is that most people have one and they are relatively inexpensive.

However, in the same way that you can make an engine more efficient by Crypton tuning it, there are things you can do to get the best out of a modem/telephone line Internet connection.

Broken Connections

Your ISP plays a vital role. If its equipment isn't up to scratch or fails for any reason, then you will have problems through no fault of your own. If you experience regular problems then consider changing your ISP.

Let's start with your gateway to the Net – the Internet Service Provider (ISP). Not all ISPs were created equal – some are definitely more reliable than others and if you are suffering from an abnormal number of disconnections, this is one of the first things to consider. No matter how many tweaks you make to your computer, if your ISP is unreliable, you will be unable to resolve this problem. Have a chat with friends and neighbors and see if any of them are using the same ISP, and if so, whether they are experiencing the same problems. There are also any number of Internet-related magazines which publish useful guides to the various ISPs' performance levels.

A common cause of broken connections is having other devices connected to the phone line you are using. These can be telephones, fax machines, answering machines or even another computer. Whenever a call comes in, these devices will be activated and will often cause the connection to be lost.

In theory, Idle Disconnect won't activate until your computer has been completely inactive for the specified period. In practice, however, it doesn't always realize that you are using the computer.

Idle Disconnect can be useful if you forget you're hooked up and you're running up your phone bill unnecessarily. This is what it is designed to prevent.

Most ISPs will automatically cut you off after a certain period, typically two hours. This eliminates the need for Idle Disconnect to a certain extent.

In the same way that a suddenly activated answering or fax machine can interfere with a connection, so can certain programs on your computer. Favorite contenders here are antivirus programs, screen-savers and Advanced Power Management (APM). All these applications, when enabled, will suddenly "kick" in and can cause a connection to be broken.

Idle Disconnect

Another common cause of broken connections is Idle Disconnect. If this occurs your modem keeps disconnecting after a certain period which is always the same. To resolve this do the following:

1 Go to Start, Control Panel, Phone and Modem Options

2 On the Modems tab, click your modem, then click Properties. Click the Advanced tab and then click Change Default Preferences. This opens the General tab

3 Here, Idle Disconnect has been enabled and is configured to break your connection after 30 minutes of inactivity. To prevent this remove the checkmark which will disable the feature

Call Waiting

This puts a modem in listening mode so that it is waiting for incoming calls. If one arrives it can break your connection.

1 Go to Start, Control Panel, Phone and Modem Options

2 Under the Dialing Rules tab click Edit

3 Check the Disable box then OK

Boost Your Browsing Speed

When using the Internet there are times when your browser will seem to be speeding along quite nicely. It may not be a match for your neighbor's Broadband connection, but it will be quite adequate for your needs.

However, there will be other times when it seems to have taken on all the characteristics of a South American tree sloth. It will literally inch along and at times even stop altogether giving you a "Connection timed out" message.

If your mouse has a center wheel for scrolling, you can change font size on the fly when viewing a Web page. To do so press and hold Ctrl while scrolling down to enlarge the font size. Scroll up to reduce the font size.

Whether or not you can do anything about this when it happens is really dependent on what's causing the slowdown, i.e. is something wrong with your PC or is the problem somewhere out on the network? Before you go fiddling with your computer's settings, this is something you need to establish.

One of the first things to check is your connection speed. Do this by clicking the "flashing monitors" icon on the right of the Taskbar and referring to the dialog which appears. If the connection is slower than normal, you will know immediately that the problem lies either with your PC or the ISP you are using. On the other hand, if it is normal, then either the site you are trying to access or the network it's on is experiencing unusual amounts of traffic which are slowing everything down. Try accessing some of your favorite sites (you'll know from experience their usual loading speed). If these are slow as well then you've just logged on at a bad time (this usually occurs in the evenings and at weekends when everyone else logs on).

You will from time to time access a site which may be extremely pretty to look at with lots of graphics and various effects. However, all this extra "baggage" will cause the site to load at a painfully slow speed. This is basically poor design as most people will quickly lose interest and move on before the page has loaded completely.

In this situation there is little you can do other than try again later. One thing you can do, however, is to disable some of your browser's media capabilities. Graphics and sound files are the slowest loading elements in a Web page (text is the quickest). If you aren't exploring graphics-rich sites, this could be a solution.

1 On your browser's menu bar select Tools, Internet Options

2 Open the Advanced tab

You will now see a dialog box offering a whole range of settings for your browser.

If you suspect that your ISP is the cause of the problem, then ditch it quickly. There's no shortage of ISPs. Open an account with another one.

Also bear in mind the cost of your Internet connection. If you are using one of the totally free ISPs then you needn't expect to achieve the highest connection speeds. This type of ISP is usually under-equipped in terms of the physical resources needed to provide a reliable service.

3 By removing the checkmarks from the appropriate boxes under Multimedia, disable some or all of the following:

- Play animations in web pages
- Play sounds in web pages
- Play videos in web pages
- Show pictures

You should now find that pages load considerably quicker than they did before, one of the main reasons being that you won't now be downloading all those irritating banner ads which are one of the main factors in a slow-loading Web page.

Check your modem settings

There are various settings which can affect the speed at which your modem operates. The first thing to do is check that your modem is configured correctly and is operating on a suitable COM port. Consult your modem documentation to find out what the settings should be and make sure they are correctly entered in the Phone and Modem Options applet in the Control Panel.

The driver that your modem is using plays a vital part in its performance.
Check that it is using the correct driver in the Device Manager. Go to Start, Control Panel and System. Click the Hardware tab and then Device Manager. Locate the modem category and click the + sign next to it. Now you will see your modem. Right click it and select Properties. In the new dialog box click Driver and then Update Driver. XP will now install the best driver for the device.

Make sure Modem is set
to the right COM port

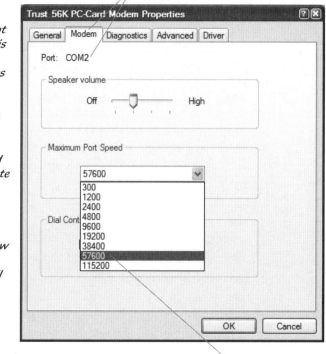

2 Set the Maximum Port Speed setting
to match that of your modem

The second thing to do is to check that the modem is using the correct driver. The thing to remember here is that while modems will often work with an incorrect driver, they may not be performing at their best.

Backup Your Internet Favorites

The Favorites application is very popular and is one of Internet Explorer's most useful features. Finding stuff on the Internet can be like looking for the proverbial needle in a haystack and having found it at last, you don't want to promptly go and lose it. This is all too easy to do given the labyrinthine structure of the Net and the way one link leads to another and then yet another and so on. Before you know where you are you have completely lost the place you started out from.

XP also provides two methods of backing up your Favorites folder, among others. These are the Files And Settings Transfer Wizard and its Backup utility. In general though, both of these methods are better suited to full system backups.

Internet Favorites solves this problem by providing a method of instantly recording the location of a particular page of interest. Having done so, you can then follow any links from that page safe in the knowledge that you can always recall the original page.

However, as with any computerized data, there is always the risk of losing it, as can happen if your hard drive goes bad for example. Therefore, if you have a large collection of Favorite links, it is a good idea to back them up so you always have a separate copy.

All you have to do is locate the Windows folder in which they are stored and then copy them to a backup folder which preferably will be on a separate drive such as a floppy disk.

Do it as follows:

1   Go to your hard drive and find a folder called Documents and Settings. Open this and you will see several more folders, the one you want is named Owner

2   Open the Owner folder and amongst others, you will now see a folder with a star-shaped icon. This is the Favorites folder

3   All you have to do is copy its contents to a backup folder you have created elsewhere

4   If you should ever need to restore the Favorites folder, then simply copy the contents of the backup folder back to the original Favorites folder

File Sharing

For those of you not yet in the know, File Sharing or Peer to Peer Networking, as it's also known, is one of the Internet's fastest growing applications. It makes use of specialized networks and software which allow computer users to connect directly to the computers of other users in the same network. The purpose of it all lies in the name – file sharing, which really says it all. Each user can designate certain files on their PC which they are willing to share.

A major problem with file sharing software occurs when a download is broken off for some reason. With many file sharing programs, you will simply have to restart again from the beginning.

This problem is exacerbated by ISPs who impose a maximum connection time (typically two hours) before automatically breaking the connection. However, some of the better programs, such as Winmx and Morpheous, can resume a download from the point at which it was broken off.

Although peer-to-peer networking is nothing new, being nearly as old as the Internet itself, its use for the purpose of file sharing most definitely is. It really took off when the Napster network came into being, a network for which specialized software was developed. This made it easy to search out and download music over the Internet. Needless to say the music industry was none too impressed and wasted little time in closing Napster down.

However, as is the way with these things, it wasn't long before others sprang up to take Napster's place. Moreover, many of these new networks took the concept a stage further and made it possible to share literally any type of file.

There are now numerous applications of this type available, with more coming along all the time. The necessary software is freely available on the Internet either directly from the manufacturer's website or from download sites such as www.download.com.

Once downloaded, all you have to do is install the program and then go through a short setting up routine. Some will require online registration but many don't.

Once set up, you can download music, movies, pictures and even full programs such as Windows XP itself.

Ideally, you should have a Broadband connection such as Cable or DSL. Movie and Sound files in particular, can be enormous in size and take an eternity to download on a standard 56Kb connection.

The one caveat with all this is that to get the best out of file sharing, you ideally need a fast Internet connection such as Cable or DSL. Many of the available programs can be hundreds of megabytes in size and with a typical 56Kb modem connection, can literally take days to download.

There are any number of file sharing programs about at the moment, all of which are available for the asking. To find out which one is best for you, try a few out. Being small programs (typically 2 to 5Mb) they are quick to download.

Popular file share programs include Bearshare, Limewire, Morpheous and Winmx. The illustration below is taken from the Winmx search window.

1 The keywords in this example are "partition magic"

Never lose sight of the fact that for file sharing to work, everybody must participate, i.e. share their own files as well. If you don't, you will find that many users will cut you off if you try to download from them (most file share software has a mechanism which allows users to see exactly what other users are sharing with the network).

2 The Results window shows a list of files available for download. All you have to do is right click a file and select Download

3 The Download window shows you what is happening. Here you can see that one file is being downloaded while another one is in a queue waiting its turn

There is also a legal, not to mention moral, aspect to the issue of file sharing. Remember, program manufacturers like Microsoft spend millions developing their software. By downloading it from the Net and then using it, you are acting illegally. Are you really being fair to them?

Save Your Files On The Internet

If you should decide to set up an online drive for yourself via the Web Publishing Wizard, you will find that you need an MSN, Hotmail or Passport email address. If you haven't got one, then you'll also have to go through the procedure of setting one up.

Welcome to the future! What are we talking about you may be asking? It is what many in the computer industry see as the next logical development of the Internet, namely as a storage medium for data hitherto kept on a PC user's hard drive.

Apparently, many of the major software manufacturers envisage that in the not too far distant future, users will be storing their files, programs and possibly even their operating systems on the Internet and downloading them to the PC only when needed. Of course for this to become a reality, Broadband access will have to be as commonplace as telephone access is today.

As a small step in this direction XP provides users with an online drive in which they can store files of their choice. It's not a very big drive, though, being approximately 25Mb.

Setting this up is done with XP's Web Publishing Wizard, which is available on the left-hand side of any open folder under File and Folder Tasks. Unfortunately, it is a long-winded affair so we won't go into the details here, suffice to say the wizard will guide you through it and that once set up, it works fine.

Microsoft are not the only company who offer free Web storage space.

There are, in fact, any number of websites which you can visit to create an account which can then be used to upload and download files as desired. Some examples are:

www.filesanywhere.com

www.zxmail.com

www.mydocsonline.com

www.myspace.com

You may be asking yourself if there is any real point to this. After all, these days 25Mb is not much in the way of storage capacity. The answer is yes, actually there is.

To start with, by using file compression software (available with XP), you can potentially turn that 25Mb into some 50Mb. Also, remember that one 1.44Mb floppy disk can hold a full-length novel, so 50Mb does actually give you something to play with.

Web storage space is also extremely secure, more so in fact, than your hard drive. It will never fail and thus is a perfect place to store really critical files.

Another major advantage is that of access. You will be able to access your online drive from any computer anywhere in the world. It doesn't take much imagination to see how this could have major implications when it comes to business usage.

Don't Let Internet Explorer Hog Your Hard Drive

By default, Internet Explorer reserves a percentage of your hard disk space for the Temporary Internet Files folder. This is where it stores copies of Web pages accessed during your browsing sessions. This is typically around 3% to 4%.

In days of old when hard drives were much smaller in terms of capacity, this percentage wouldn't have amounted to all that much. However, given the huge sizes of today's drives, you can now be completely wasting some 700Mb of a 20Gb drive, for example.

You can claim this space back by doing the following:

1   Go to Start, Control Panel, Internet Options

2   On the General tab, click Settings. This opens the Settings dialog box

While in Settings, you can view the contents of the Temporary Internet Files folder, you can specify a different folder to be used for this purpose and you will be able to configure the way Internet Explorer updates stored pages.

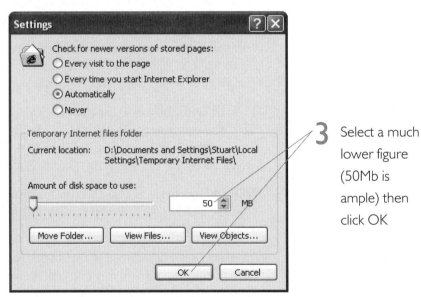

3   Select a much lower figure (50Mb is ample) then click OK

Should you ever find that the amount you have allocated to Internet Explorer isn't enough, then you can easily up it a bit.

How Old is That Web Page?

The Internet is certainly a mine of information concerning just about every subject known to man. However, just as books eventually become dated unless periodically revised, so do all those millions of web pages.

You can instantly find out how current are the contents of any book simply by looking at the date of publication inside the front cover. Very few websites, though, offer any guide in this respect and so the surfer may well be reading content that is in fact years out of date and so will in many cases be completely useless.

However, there is a way to determine how old a web page is and you can do it as follows:

1 Open the relevant page in your browser

It is a bit of a pain to have to type this into your browser every time you want to check a page. A good idea is to type it into a Notepad document and then drag the document to the Links toolbar on your browser. Then you can just open the Notepad document and copy/paste the command into your browser.

2 In the address box type the following:

javascript:alert(document.lastModified)

Microsoft PowerToys for Windows XP - Microsoft Internet Explorer

File   Edit   View   Favorites   Tools   Help   Links Google Stu Update

Back   Forward   Stop   Refresh   Home   Search   Favorites   History   Mail   Print   Edit

Address   javascript:alert(document.lastModified)   Go

3 Hit Enter on your keyboard or the browser Go button

4 Now you will see a dialog box open up and inside it will be the date and time the page was last updated

Microsoft Internet Explorer

⚠ 10/18/2002 16:10:42

OK

This tip will work with any web page and will enable the surfer to find out just how current the information he or she is reading actually is.

Power Surfing

This is a very simple yet extremely effective tip for those of you who like to surf the web using search engines as a starting point.

When doing this most people simply click on a link that interests them and when finished with it use the back button to return to the search engine. This is satisfactory but there is in fact a much better way to do it.

Instead of opening one browser window, open two. Then right click on the taskbar and choose Tile Windows Vertically. Now adjust the size of the two browser windows so that the one on the left is about three inches wide and the other fills the rest of the screen. This is demonstrated below.

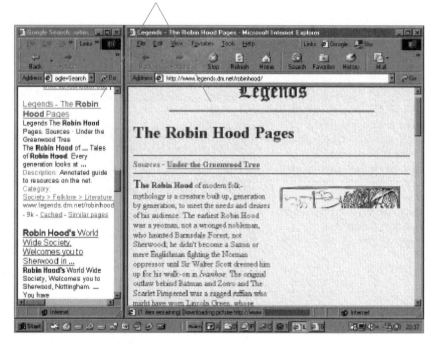

Open the search engine in the smaller window and then simply drag a link that interests you into the bigger one. Now you can browse whilst having your list of links in view at all times. To open a new link just drag it into the main window. No more constantly hitting the Back button.

Internet Explorer Key Shortcuts

 As with general Windows applications, the keyboard can also be used to control Internet Explorer.

ALT+MINUS	Zoom out.
ALT+PLUS	Zoom in.
F11	Toggle between full-screen and regular views of the browser window.
ESC	Stop downloading a page.
ALT+P	Set printing options and print the page.
ALT+D	Select the text in the Address bar.
CTRL+A	Select all items on the current Web page.
DOWN ARROW	Scroll toward the end of a document.
PAGE DOWN	Scroll toward the end of a document in larger increments.
UP ARROW	Scroll toward the beginning of a document.
PAGE UP	Scroll toward the beginning of a document in larger increments.
CTRL+S	Save the current page.
CTRL+X	Remove the selected items and copy them to the Clipboard.
CTRL+F5	Refresh the current Web page.
CTRL+P	Print the current page or active frame.
CTRL+E	Open the Search bar.
CTRL+B	Open the Organize Favorites dialog box.
CTRL+H	Open the History bar.
CTRL+I	Open the Favorites bar.
CTRL+N	Open a new window.
END	Move to the end of a document.
HOME	Move to the beginning of a document.
UP ARROW	Move forward through the list of AutoComplete matches.
TAB	Move forward through the items on a Web page, the Address bar, and the Links bar.
DOWN ARROW	Move back through the list of AutoComplete matches.
CTRL+V	Insert the contents of the Clipboard at the selected location.
CTRL+Click	In the History or Favorites bars, open multiple folders.

ALT+HOME	Go to your Home page.
BACKSPACE	Go to the previous page.
ALT+RIGHT ARROW	Go to the next page.
CTRL+O or CTRL+L	Go to a new location.
CTRL+F	Find on this page.
ALT+LEFT ARROW	Display the previous page to be printed.
ALT+RIGHT ARROW	Display the next page to be printed.
ALT+END	Display the last page to be printed.
ALT+HOME	Display the first page to be printed.
F1	Display Internet Explorer Help or (when in a dialog box) display context Help on an item.
SHIFT+F10	Display a shortcut menu for a link.
ALT+Z	Display a list of zoom percentages.
F4	Display a list of addresses you've typed.
CTRL+C	Copy the selected items to the Clipboard.
CTRL+W	Close the current window.
ALT+C	Close Print Preview.
CTRL+D	Add the current page to your Favorites.
CTRL+ENTER	Add www. to the beginning and .com to the end of the text typed in the Address bar.
ENTER	Activate a selected link.
CTRL+RIGHT ARROW	When in the Address bar, move the cursor right to the next logical break in the address (period or slash).
CTRL+LEFT ARROW	When in the Address bar, move the cursor left to the next logical break in the address (period or slash).
ALT+F	Specify how you want frames to print. This option is available only if you are printing a Web page that uses frames.
CTRL+F5	Refresh the current Web page, even if the time stamp for the Web and locally stored versions are the same.

Security

Security on a PC ranges from keeping private files safe from access by others, and keeping your system free of viruses to hiding your Internet browsing tracks. This chapter covers all these issues and more.

Covers

Chapter Seven

Dangerous Email Attachments

Email is a lot of fun and also very useful. For many people it is one of the primary uses of their computer. However, like most good things it has a downside.

This comes in the form of viruses which are commonly transmitted via email in the form of an attachment to the email message. This is indicated by a paper clip symbol. Usually the message will be enticingly worded to encourage the recipient to have a look. This is for the simple reason that before the virus can be released the attachment must be opened. If it isn't then nothing will happen. A message of this type is demonstrated in the following illustration:

Whenever you receive an email with an attachment, take a look at the attachment's file extension. This will give you a very good indication as to whether the attachment is safe to open or not.

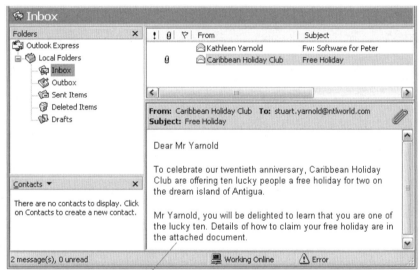

The only way an attachment can release a virus into your system is if you open it.

If you receive a message like this, regard it with immediate suspicion. The odds are that it is just a harmless mailshot but there is a always a possibility that someone has sent you a virus.

A good way of determining the likelihood of an attachment containing a virus is by looking at its file extension.

If the file extension is .exe, .com, .bat, .pif, .scr, or .vbs, be extremely wary. These extensions belong to programs and scripts that can carry a deadly virus. If, on the other hand, the extension is .gif, .jpg, or .wav, you're OK.

If the extension is .doc or .xls, the file is an Office document that may contain macros.

Don't be fooled by multiple extensions – the ILOVEYOU virus, for example, is called LOVE-LETTER-FOR-YOU.TXT.vbs. The only extension that counts is the very last one, immediately following the final dot.

While it does no harm to err on the side of caution when it comes to viruses, it is a fact that there is a lot of scaremongering regarding this subject. The reality is that the majority of people will run a PC all their lives without getting one. Keep the issue in proportion.

Click the paperclip symbol

Inbox

Folders	×
Outlook Express	
Local Folders	
Inbox	
Outbox	
Sent Items	
Deleted Items	
Drafts	

!	0	⏷	From	Subject
			Kathleen Yarnold	Fw: Software for Peter
	0		Caribbean Holiday Club	Free Holiday

From: Caribbean Holiday Club **To:** stuart.yarnold@ntlworld.com
Subject: Free Holiday

Dear Mr Yarnold

Holiday details.doc (21.5 KB)

Save Attachments...

To celebrate our twentieth anniversary, Caribbean Holiday Club are offering ten lucky people a free holiday for two on the dream island of Antigua.

Mr Yarnold, you will be delighted to learn that you are one of the lucky ten. Details of how to claim your free holiday are in the attached document.

Contacts ▼	×
There are no contacts to display. Click on Contacts to create a new contact.	

2 message(s), 0 unread   Working Online   ⚠ Error

2 This will reveal the name of the file, its size and its extension. In the above example the extension is .doc which indicates it is an Office document

If you are in any doubt at all, run a virus checker before opening the attachment. Be aware though, that as new viruses are being written all the time, it is vital that your antivirus program is kept up-to-date. You can do this by downloading updates from the manufacturer's website.

Hide Your Browsing Tracks

Another thing for the privacy-minded to be aware of is their Internet Favorites. Certain sites when accessed will automatically add a link to their site to your Favorites folder. Common culprits in this respect are porn sites (again, don't ask how I know this). Your Internet Favorites can be accessed from the Menu Bar in most windows and anyone who happens to do this will see anything which has been added in this way.

As anybody who regularly browses the Internet will know, it can be all too easy to stumble across some of the Web's less salubrious content. You may have entered something completely innocent in the search box only to be regaled by something you definitely didn't expect. For example, you may have been looking for information on the pop singer Britney Spears only to bring up an extremely explicit site regarding a porn star of the same name (don't ask how the author knows about this).

Unfortunately (in the above scenario), XP, along with other versions of Windows, keeps a record of what you have been doing on the Internet.

On your hard drive, there exist three folders which contain information relating to your browsing activities:

The three folders that can give the game away for you are the Temporary Internet Files, History and Cookie folders.

- The first is the Cookies folder which can be found in Documents and User Settings\Owner\Cookies. Cookies are small programs which many sites will automatically download to your PC and which give them basic information about you e.g. the last time you visited that site

- Second, there is the Temporary Internet Files folder which is basically a cache of the pages you have accessed. Should you revisit a particular site, instead of pulling it off the Web your browser will retrieve it from this cache. This makes access to the page much quicker

- Third, you have the History folder which your browser uses to keep track of the websites you have visited. You will find both the Temporary Internet Files and History folders in Documents and Settings\Owner\Local Settings

Anyone who knows how can access these folders and see exactly what you have been up to on the Internet.

One way to prevent this is to open each of the folders and manually delete their contents at the end of each browsing session.

There is however, an easier way and this is as follows:

> Go to Start, Control Panel and Internet Options

...cont'd

2 This will open Internet Options at the General tab as shown below:

Click the Advanced tab of Internet Options and you will be presented with a whole range of further options. Scroll down towards the bottom of the list to an option for the automatic clearing of the "Temporary Internet Files" folder when the browser is closed.

This is worth selecting as nothing in this folder is worth keeping, indeed all it does is take up valuable space on your hard drive.

3 You can delete all existing Cookies and Temporary Internet Files here

4 Clear the History folder by clicking this button

5 Set the number of days to keep items in the History folder here

6 Click the Privacy tab

7 Using the slider you can adjust the types of Cookie that your browser will accept

Turn Off Auto Complete

Be careful when using Auto Complete. Not only can it automatically enter your passwords and user names for other people to use illicitly, it can also enable people to see exactly what sites you have been visiting and what keywords you have been entering in search engine search boxes.

Internet Explorer has a feature called Auto Complete which when enabled causes the browser to automatically save Web addresses, user names, passwords and data entered on Web-based forms. This can be convenient as it saves the user from having to type out this information each time.

However, it can also be dangerous in that it potentially allows other people to access your password-protected pages and see what data you've entered in forms etc. It will also enable any snooper to see exactly what websites you have visited and any keywords entered in search engine search boxes.

Probably for most people this isn't a problem but if you wish to keep this type of information private then you need to disable Auto Complete or alter its settings. This can be done as follows:

The safest way to use Auto Complete is to disable the User names and passwords on forms option. Enabling it to remember Web addresses is safe and can be very useful.

1 Open Internet Explorer, go to the Tools menu and select Internet Options, Content.

2 In the new window, under Personal information, click the Auto Complete button

When you disable any of Auto Complete's settings as in step 3, it will "forget" any information it previously held regarding this setting.

AutoComplete Settings [?][X]

AutoComplete lists possible matches from entries you've typed before.

Use AutoComplete for
- ☑ Web addresses
- ☐ Forms
- ☑ User names and passwords on forms
  - ☑ Prompt me to save passwords

Clear AutoComplete history

[Clear Forms]   [Clear Passwords]

To clear Web address entries, on the General tab in Internet Options, click Clear History.

[OK]   [Cancel]

3 Here you can choose whether or not to use the feature for Web addresses, Forms and User names and passwords

4 To get rid of existing entries, you can click the Clear Forms and Clear Passwords buttons

Censor Available Web Content

Many people, with good reason, are wary of letting their children loose on the Internet unsupervised. There can't be many who aren't aware of the dangers posed by chatrooms and various other types of site.

So the responsible parent will want to be sure their children are not accessing things they shouldn't be. How to do it though?

One way is to sit with them, which can be excruciating if all they want to do is catch up with the latest adventures of Britney Spears for example.

A less painful way is to make use of XP's Content Advisor which is also available from Internet Options under the Content tab. Click Enable and you will see the following:

While Contents Advisor does a reasonable job, it isn't the best application of its type. Enabling it can cause sites with absolutely no offensive content at all to be blocked.
  Much better programs include "Net Nanny" and "Cyber Patrol".

2 Select the Approved Sites tab to specify accessible sites

3 Select the General tab to password-protect the Contents Advisor so no-one can override your settings

Content Advisor

Ratings | Approved Sites | General | Advanced

Select a category to view the rating levels:

- RSACi
  - Language
  - Nudity
  - Sex
  - Violence

Adjust the slider to specify what users are allowed to see:

Level 2:   Moderate expletives

Description

Expletives; non-sexual anatomical references.

To view the Internet page for this rating service, click More Info.

More Info...

OK | Cancel | Apply

| Drag the slider to set the level of permissible content

Hide Your Private Files Away

There are any number of reasons why someone might wish to hide a folder. It might, for example, contain important work documents or a set of financial accounts.

XP does provide a method of securely encrypting a folder, but unfortunately this feature is only available with the Professional version. In any case it doesn't actually hide the folder itself. So anyone can stumble across a password-protected folder and while they won't be able to access it, they will know it might contain something important. In effect it's been "signposted" as such. The point here is that, to someone in the know, there are methods of cracking passwords.

Another way to hide a folder is to simply squirrel it away in a folder containing a mass of other folders or sub-folders. Just don't forget where it is.

Another option is to simply conceal the existence of the folder and this can be done as follows:

1 Right click the folder to be hidden and select Properties. On the General tab check the Hidden box

2 Open any folder and from the menu bar select Tools, Folder Options. In the new window select Views

The method described on this page, while useful, is by no means a secure one. Anyone who knows how to access hidden folders will be able to access your hidden ones as well.

3 Select Do not show hidden files or folders

The next time the drive containing your folder is opened, the folder will not be visible. To access it simply undo step 3 above.

Banish Hackers

When you are browsing the Internet, you are in fact browsing the content of other computers. That's what the Internet is – a network of linked computers. In the same way, it's quite possible for other computer users to access yours.

You will only be a target for hackers if you have a Broadband Internet connection such as Cable or DSL. Even then it's unlikely. Unless you keep information such as credit card details on the computer, it's not an issue that should concern you.

If you do however, then XP's Internet Connection Firewall will be a useful thing to have.

For someone to do this (these people are known as "hackers") they need skills that the average user just doesn't possess. It's also true to say that if your Internet access is via a telephone line, it's extremely unlikely to happen to you. For a start you are unlikely to be online for a long enough period.

However, should you be one of the growing number of people now using Broadband for Internet access, your connection will be permanent and for much of the time your PC will be unattended. In this situation you are much more likely to be hacked.

The traditional method of protection against hacking is by what's known as a firewall. These things basically work by making a PC invisible to would-be hackers. If they don't know it's there, they can't hack it.

Unlike previous versions of Windows, XP provides users with an in-built firewall called Internet Connection Firewall (ICF).

Setting up Internet Connection Firewall

1 Go to Start, Control Panel, Network Connections

2 Select your connection and then, under Network Tasks, click Change settings of this connection

3 On the Advanced tab, under Internet Connection Firewall, select the Protect my computer and network by limiting or preventing access to this computer from the Internet check box

4 Your PC will now be safe from those nasty hackers

Keep Your Account Password Safe

This tip presumes you have set a password for your User Account (User Profile in previous Windows versions).

It is a fact that passwords are notoriously easy to forget, particularly if you have set passwords for several different computer applications. You may actually have quite a few to remember.

In the case of your User Account, XP gives you an option for saving your password lest you forget it. This is how to do it:

This tip will require a blank, formatted floppy disk.

1 Go to Start, Control Panel, User Accounts. Click the account for which you wish to save the password. In the new window you'll see a range of options, including (on the far left) Related Tasks

Keep your password-reset disk in a safe place. If someone else gets hold of it they will be able to access your account by simply setting a new password which will supersede the previous one. Not only that, but you will then be unable to access your own account.

2 Click Prevent a forgotten password

3 A special wizard launches – simply follow the steps

4 If you enter the incorrect password when logging on, a pop-up message will appear saying "Did you forget your password?". You can use your password-reset disk. Click Use your password reset disk and a recovery wizard will prompt you to insert your recovery disk in the floppy drive. You will now be able to set a new password which will override the original

Lock Your Computer Quickly

The tip on this page will only work if you have a password protected User Account set up on the computer.

To unlock the PC you will need the password for that particular account.

An occasion might arise when you are in the middle of an important task on the computer, when for some reason you are called away in a hurry for what will probably be a short period. You haven't got time to save the work and switch off but you absolutely don't want to leave it unattended in case someone comes along and meddles with it while you're away.

There is a quick and foolproof way round this problem:

1 Right-click the Desktop, select New and then Shortcut

2 In the location of item box, type the following:

   rundll32.exe user32.dll,LockWorkStation

If you have Fast User Switching enabled, instead of getting the "This computer is in use and has been locked" window, you will be taken to the log on screen. The effect will be the same though. The PC will be locked and will need the password to unlock it.

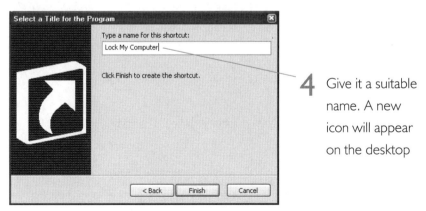

3 Click Next

If you don't want to go to the bother of creating a special icon to lock the computer, you can achieve the same thing simply by pressing the Windows key on the keyboard in conjunction with the letter L.

4 Give it a suitable name. A new icon will appear on the desktop

To lock your PC instantly, all you have to do is click the icon.

Override Your BIOS Password

The BIOS is a chip on the motherboard which carries out all the initialization routines required to boot a computer and then load the operating system.

The BIOS can be accessed by the user (usually by hitting the Del key on the keyboard just after the PC is switched on). This takes the user into the BIOS setup program from where it is possible to make many configuration alterations to your system's hardware. In certain troubleshooting situations, BIOS access is very useful.

The keyboard entry required to enter the BIOS setup program can be found at the bottom of the screen as the PC starts. Usually it is the DEL key but on some computers it may be different.

However, the setup program has a facility for password-protecting BIOS access and this is very often enabled by PC manufacturers to prevent users poking around in it. If you don't know what this password is, you're basically stymied.

Should you ever find yourself in this situation, try the following:

1   Reboot the computer to an A:\> prompt by using an old Windows startup disk

Be careful with what changes you make in the BIOS. As with the Registry, it's possible to mess up your system.

If you're unsure of something you've done here, look for an entry that says Load defaults or something similar. This will undo any changes you have made.

2   At the prompt type "debug" then hit Enter

3   Now you will see a "_" at the debug prompt

4   Type "o 70 2e" at the debug prompt which will show as "_o 70 2e" then hit Enter again

5   Now type "o 71 ff" and hit Enter again

6   Finally, type "q" and hit Enter one last time

7   Reboot your computer, access the bootup setup program and the password box will have disappeared

Secure Your PC

Should a XP user ever wish to ensure that absolutely nobody can enter his or her computer, they can do so by using what is known as *Securing the Windows XP Account Database*. To enable this do the following:

1   Go to Start, Run and in the box type "syskey". This opens the following dialog box. Click Update

Once you have secured the PC as detailed in this tip, you cannot undo it. So beforehand consider carefully whether or not you really need this level of security.

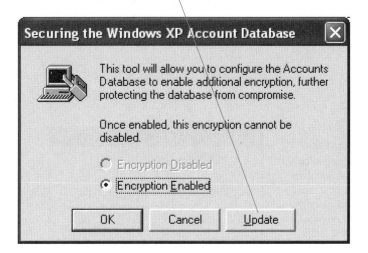

2   The next dialog box offers you two main options as shown below

The first option is to set a password. Once this has been done, every time the computer is started, a window will appear before the logon screen, requesting the password be entered. Without it nobody can log on, not even the administrator. To do this simply enter and re-enter a password as shown in the illustration in Step 2. Click OK and you will get a confirmation message.

The second method is to create an encrypted key that can be stored either on a floppy disk or as a file in the system. Do this as described below:

1 Check System Generated Password and then check Store Startup Key on Floppy Disk. Click OK

While the floppy disk method may be the more secure of the two, it will only be so as long as the disk itself is secure. Should it fall into the wrong hands then it's actually an open invitation. Furthermore, should it be lost or become damaged, which floppies are prone to, then you will be locked out of your own PC.

Startup Key ☒

○ Password Startup
  Requires a password to be entered during system start.

  Password: [   ]
  Confirm: [   ]

● System Generated Password

  ● Store Startup Key on Floppy Disk
    Requires a floppy disk to be inserted during system start.

  ○ Store Startup Key Locally
    Stores a key as part of the operating system, and no interaction is required during system start.

  [OK]   [Cancel]

2 You will now be asked to insert a floppy disk after which an encrypted key will be saved to the disk

From this point on, every time the computer is started, you will be asked to insert the disk into the floppy drive before you can access the logon screen. So just make sure you don't lose it otherwise you won't be able to access your own computer.

Password Protect Your Files

XP allows individual files and folders to be encrypted should you wish to keep their contents private. However, to make use of this facility, you need to format your hard drive with the NTFS file system which not everybody will want to do. See page 152.

However, there is still a way to protect your data without using the NTFS system and this can be done by password protection. The procedure for setting this up is as follows:

1 Right click the desktop and select New, Compressed (zipped) Folder. Give it a suitable name

2 Place the files you wish to password protect into the compressed folder

3 Open the folder and from the File menu select Add a Password

This tip will only work with XP's compressed folders.

4 In the Add Password dialog box, enter your password and then click OK

5 Should you ever want to change or remove the password, simply select Remove Password from the File menu

Create a MS-DOS Startup Disk

Startup disks from previous versions of Windows contain the following tools:

Chkdisk.exe	Performs basic disk diagnostics.
Scandisk.exe	Performs basic disk diagnostics and repairs.
Fdisk.exe	Performs reformatting tasks on your hard drive.
Uninstall.exe	Uninstalls Windows from your PC.

However, XP's startup disc contains none of the above tools — it simply takes you to a DOS prompt. If you wish to run any of the above tools on an XP system, you can, though, use a previous Windows startup disk.

Previous versions of Windows allow the user to create a startup disk from the Add/Remove Programs Control Panel applet. The startup disk enables a user to boot his or her computer into a DOS mode which gives them limited access to the PC if for any reason Windows wouldn't start. The disk also contains diagnostic, repair and setup tools.

With XP, the option to make a startup disk is missing from the Add/Remove Programs applet.

It is, however, still possible to make one in XP. Do it as follows:

1 Place a floppy disk in the floppy drive

2 Go to My Computer and right click the floppy drive

3 From the menu, select Format

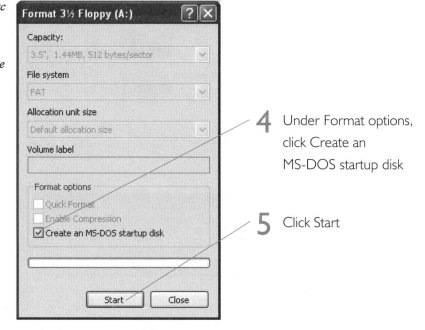

4 Under Format options, click Create an MS-DOS startup disk

5 Click Start

Installation/Setting Up

All components in a computer system have first to be installed and set up before they can be used to their full potential. This applies to both hardware and software.

For many, the installation procedure will be simplicity itself with little or no setting up required. Other applications, such as Windows, require a bit more attention. Also, many applications come with useful features that are either disabled by default or need configuring correctly.

This chapter shows you how.

Covers

Chapter Eight

Trouble-free XP Installation

Before carrying out a Windows installation, make sure you have backed up any data you don't wish to lose. While it's rare, new installations can result in the loss of data.

Although XP, along with other recent versions of Windows, will normally install without too many problems, there will always be occasions when it doesn't. This isn't due to anything inherently wrong with XP's installation program but rather will usually be the result of the user not taking a few simple precautionary measures beforehand. These are as follows:

1 Optimize your hard drive by running Windows Disk Defragmenter which will rearrange the data on your drive into a neat and orderly pattern

2 Run Chkdsk to check your drive for any errors. Drive errors are a common cause of failed installations

It is important to uninstall or disable any antivirus software you have on your system prior to installing XP.

3 Run a virus check on your system. In the unlikely event of one being present, it would be foolish to transfer it to a new setup

4 Having ascertained that your system is free of viruses, uninstall the virus checking program. Alternatively, it can be disabled via the BIOS setup program. Virus checkers are another common cause of installation problems

When carrying out an installation, although not essential, it is a good idea to disconnect as much of your system hardware as you can. Examples are printers, scanners and modems. The reason for this is that it is during the hardware detection and configuration stages of an installation, that problems often crop up.

5 Disable any applications that run in the background and can suddenly activate. Examples of these are screensavers, antivirus programs as mentioned above and utility programs such as Norton's System Works

6 It's also a good idea to remove all programs from your Startup folder. These are programs which start automatically as Windows is loading

Carrying out the above steps will almost certainly enable you to install XP without a hitch.

How To Do a Clean XP Installation

When installing any version of Windows you have two ways to do it. The first is to simply install the new version over the existing version. This is known as an upgrade and is the option taken by most people.

The best way to install any operating system is by doing a clean installation. There will be much less risk of problems and it will also be much quicker.

The second option is to do a "clean" installation and is definitely the better of the two. To do it you first have to format the hard drive and this procedure literally wipes the drive clean. Not only will this clear the drive of all previously held data but it will also clear it of anything that might interfere with the installation procedure. Do it as follows:

Should you not have an old startup disk, you can carry out a hard drive format (and partitioning, if necessary) from the XP installation disk.

1 First, make a backup copy of all your important files as the format procedure will destroy the existing ones

2 Locate the Startup disk from your previous version of Windows and insert it into the floppy drive. Then reboot the PC

3 After a few moments you will be presented with a list of three options. Using the arrow keys, select option two – Start Computer without CD-ROM Support

4 After a minute or two you will see a list of entries which ends in the A:\> command prompt. Type "FORMAT C:". The finished entry should look like this "A:\>FORMAT C:". Then hit Enter

Scan your system for viruses before you start. In the event that you have one, it would be stupid to transfer it to your new and probably otherwise perfect setup.

5 Next you will see a message warning that all data on non-removable disk Drive C will be lost! Proceed with format (Y/N)?

6 Hit the letter Y and then Enter. The format procedure will now start and usually takes between 30 minutes and an hour

7 When the format is finished, reboot the PC and a few moments after the startup screen appears hit the Del key (on some systems you may need to use a different key – it will be specified)

All BIOS setup programs have a facility for password protection.
Many manufacturers will set a password to prevent users poking around in the BIOS, where it is possible to do a lot of damage.
If this is the case with your system refer to page 130 where you will find a way to override an existing BIOS password.

8 The BIOS setup program will now open. Using the arrow keys on the keyboard, go to BIOS Features Setup and hit Enter. Scroll down until you see an entry called Boot Sequence. You will notice that the existing sequence begins with the letter A, which is the floppy drive. Using the Page Up or Page Down keys, toggle the sequence until CD-ROM is first in the list. Hit Esc and you will be returned to the first screen. Scroll down to Save and Exit Setup, hit Enter and when you are asked to confirm by typing Y or N, type "Y"

9 Place the XP installation disk in the CD-ROM drive and then reboot the computer. XP's installation routine will now begin

A few words of explanation are in order here. Previous versions of Windows were not bootable from the CD. Thus, in order to start the setup procedure, the PC had to be booted from a floppy disk which was called a startup or boot floppy. These disks contained CD-ROM drivers which enabled the CD-ROM to be recognized by the setup program.

Your XP installation disk, unlike previous Windows installation disks, is bootable. This means you no longer have to worry about startup disks and the mysteries of DOS.
The one proviso is that the PC's boot sequence must first be set so that the CD-ROM drive is the first drive that the system accesses. Once this is done you can throw away all those old startup disks.

The XP CD though, is bootable and so startup or boot floppies are not needed. However, for CD-ROM booting to work, there is one requirement that must be met. The BIOS boot sequence must be set to begin with the CD-ROM drive, which means that this is where the BIOS will look for the operating system. If it is configured to look in the floppy drive first, which is the default setting, it won't find it. At that point things just stop. It's then up to the user to tell the BIOS that it should be looking in the CD-ROM drive by typing in an appropriate instruction at a command (DOS) prompt. This is how clean installations of previous Windows versions are done.

Once the boot sequence has been altered in the BIOS setup, future installations of XP will be a breeze. Simply place the installation disk in the CD-ROM drive and reboot the PC. Shortly into the bootup routine you will see a message at the bottom of the screen saying Press any key to boot from CD. That's all you will have to do.

Install Windows XP Fast

This tip is for the movers amongst you who like to get things done in a hurry. Basically, it entails running the Windows setup directly from your hard drive, as opposed to from your CD-ROM drive. The advantage of doing it this way is speed – a hard drive operates much quicker than a CD-ROM drive.

This tip will only work for an upgrade or reinstallation, as you will need access to Windows to start the installation procedure.

1   Create a folder on your hard drive and give it a name such as Windows Setup

2   Put the installation disc in the CD-ROM drive and open it by right clicking the drive in My Computer and selecting Open. From Edit on the menu bar, click Select All and then Copy

An added bonus to installing XP in this way is that you will never be asked to insert the Windows CD as you sometimes are when installing certain applications. An example is when using the Add/Remove Programs applet in the Control Panel to install extra Windows components.

3   Go back to the new folder you have just created on the hard drive, open it and from Edit on the menu bar, select Paste. The entire contents of the installation CD will be copied to this folder. When the procedure is finished the folder will look like this:

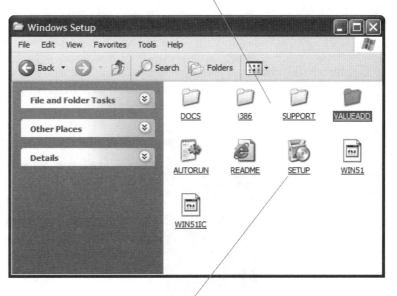

Copying the contents of the installation disc will take up just under 500Mb of your hard drive space. If this is space you can't afford or don't want to lose, then you can just delete the Setup folder once the installation is complete.

4   For an express XP installation, all you have to do is click Setup

Dual Boot With XP

Dual booting is a facility which, with XP, is available for the first time to Windows users without the need to install third-party software.

If you choose to set up dual booting on your computer, make sure that XP is the last operating system to be installed.

Dual booting allows two or more operating systems to be installed on a computer and thus the user has a choice as to which system he wants to run. As with all things though, dual booting has its advantages and also its disadvantages.

Each installed operating system must be on a separate drive or partition of a drive. If you try to install XP on a drive that already contains a previous version of Windows, it will simply overwrite the existing files.

One of the first things to realize is that each installed operating system must be on a separate hard drive. If you already have two or more drives then you're all set. Even if you don't, however, you can still make use of dual booting. To do this though, you will need to first partition your hard drive. This basically means that your drive is split into two sections or partitions, each of which appears to Windows as a separate drive.

This issue of partitioning is a complicated one and is beyond the scope of this book to adequately address. However, there is no shortage of reading matter on this subject in the bookstores not to mention computer magazines and on the Internet where you will find all the information you need.

So, having got your two drives, be they partitions or individual drives, you are now ready to set up dual booting facilities.

You are given the option of setting it up right at the beginning of XP's installation routine:

If you don't understand the issue of drive partitioning, fire up your Web browser, go to any search engine and type "hard drive partitioning" in the search box.

Select New Installation (Advanced) and click Next

One huge advantage of a dual boot system is that should one of the operating systems fail terminally, you will still have an alternative system to work with.

To install XP in a different drive or partition, as you must do to enable dual booting, you need to select the New Installation (Advanced) option at the beginning of the installation routine.

One drawback with dual booting is that if you want your programs to work with all the operating systems, you will usually need to install a copy on each drive or partition. This will mean you having two or more copies of the same programs on your computer. This is obviously going to eat up your hard drive.

The Setup routine will now begin. After 10 minutes or so Setup will reboot the computer and on restart you will be presented with a DOS screen asking you in which drive or partition you wish to install XP. Setup will automatically highlight the option it considers to be the best. This, of course, will be the drive or partition which doesn't yet have an operating system installed in it.

Go with Setup's choice and XP will now install itself in the usual manner. And that's it, there's nothing else you have to do.

From now on, every time the computer is rebooted, you will be taken to a DOS screen as shown below:

```
Please select the operating system to start:

Microsoft XP Home Edition
Microsoft Windows

Use the up and down keys to move the highlight to your choice
Press to Enter.
Seconds until highlighted choice will be started automatically: 4




For troubleshooting and advanced options for Windows press, F8
```

1 Use the Up and Down arrow keys to choose the operating system you want to run

2 Hit Enter on your keyboard and the selected operating system will now load

Setting the Default Boot System

This tip is for those who have set up their computer as a dual boot system with two or more operating systems. When this has been done and the computer is started they will be presented with a boot menu which details the available operating systems. These are selected by using the arrow keys.

The system at the top of the list is the default system and if the user hasn't made a choice in a specified number of seconds, is the one which the PC will run.

Should the user wish to set a different system as the default, this is the way to do it:

1 Right click My Computer, click Properties, click the Advanced tab and then click the Settings button under Startup and Recovery

Startup and Recovery

System startup

Default operating system:

"Microsoft Windows XP Home Edition" /fastdetect

"Microsoft Windows XP Home Edition" /fastdetect
"Microsoft Windows"

☑ Time to display recovery options when needed: 30 seconds

To edit the startup options file manually, click Edit. [Edit]

System failure

☑ Write an event to the system log
☑ Send an administrative alert
☑ Automatically restart

Write debugging information

Small memory dump (64 KB)

Small dump directory:
%SystemRoot%\Minidump

☑ Overwrite any existing file

[OK] [Cancel]

2 The drop down box will show the operating systems installed. Highlight the one you want to be the default and click OK

3 You can also alter the time available to make your choice here

Set Up XP for Several Users

A very useful and much overlooked feature of Windows in general and XP in particular, is that of setting up PC preferences and various system configurations, to suit the personal tastes and requirements of those that use the computer.

XP's User Accounts enable a PC to be personalized for any number of different users. They can each set up their account as they would if it was their own PC.

For example, Junior can have the most outlandish sound and display schemes he can find and generally have the PC set up for what he does best, such as playing games. Dad, on the other hand, might be taking advantage of something that the explosion in computer use has offered many people – namely the option of working from home. To do this, he has to set up the PC in much the same way he would have it at the office. Other members of the household can also set up the computer to suit their requirements.

To illustrate the procedure we will assume you are Dad:

1 Go to Start, Control Panel and User Accounts. You will see the following:

When more than one account is created, one of those accounts must be an Administrator account. The person running this account will be able to set restrictions on what other account holders can and can't do. For example, restrictions can be placed on which folders can be accessed, whether or not programs can be installed or uninstalled, among others.

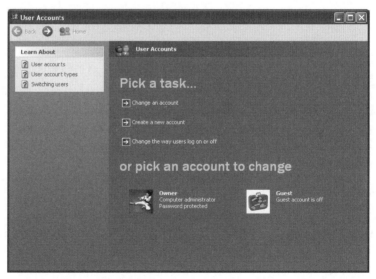

2 Dad owns the PC and, when he upgraded to XP, was prompted by the Setup routine to enter a user name. This automatically created the first User Account (Owner) which also makes it the Administrator Account. This puts Dad in overall charge of the PC

In a multi-user environment there will inevitably be occasions when one user needs to take over the PC from someone else using it. Ordinarily, this might necessitate the original user having to close down whatever he or she was working on so that the PC can be rebooted to the User Welcome screen. This will enable the new user to log on to his or her account.

To overcome this problem, XP provides a much quicker way known as "Fast User Switching". This is available by going to the User Account dialog box and clicking "Change the way users log on and off". To use it, go to Start and Log Off.

An excellent way of utilizing XP's User Accounts is for a single user to create different accounts to suit the different uses to which he or she puts the PC.

For example, one account could be created and set up for graphics editing purposes while another can be set up as a home office. All the relevant programs and folders for each can be placed on the desktop or even in the Startup folder so that they start automatically. In effect, you can have any number of personalized desktops.

3 All the settings on the PC at this stage belong to the Computer Administrator's account, i.e. Dad, and are the ones he wants. The PC is set up for him. At the moment however, anyone can come along and change those settings. To prevent this, XP allows him to set a password for the account

4 Now it's time to turn Junior loose. Dad, being the administrator, goes to the User Account dialog box, clicks Create a new account and then names it Junior. To limit the possible damage Junior can do to the PC, he elects to create a Limited account. This means that Junior is severely restricted as to what changes he can make to the PC in terms of adding/deleting software and hardware, changing account passwords and file access.

With his new account Junior can now set up the PC to suit his own peculiar tastes and requirements within the restrictions placed on him by his Limited account

5 Dad now creates further Limited accounts for anyone else who will use the PC. They, in turn, can now set up the computer for their requirements. Limited account users can also password protect their accounts

Once all the required user accounts have been set up, each time the PC is booted, a welcome screen will appear with the names of all the account holders. All they have to do is click the account and they are in. If they have elected to password protect their account, a password box will appear.

Device Driver Rollback

XP's Driver Rollback system only kicks in when you update a driver. When you do this it keeps a backup copy of the original driver. If you have subsequent problems, it will be able to replace the new driver with the one that worked.

Device drivers are small software programs which act as an interface between Windows and the associated hardware device. All devices, no matter how simple, as in the humble mouse, use them and typically these days they are supplied on a CD.

However, it is not uncommon for badly written drivers to cause problems with devices and even with the operating system.

Because of this driver fallibility problem, XP includes a Device Driver Rollback system.

Let's assume you have updated your modem driver and then found that your modem won't work any more. You've lost the original driver. Ordinarily, you would now have to do a search on the Internet which takes time even assuming you have Internet access.

Well, not any more. Device Driver Rollback will save the day. Use it as follows:

1. Go to Start, Control Panel, System, Hardware, Device Manager. Click the + sign next to the Modem category and then right click the modem. Then click Properties, and in the Properties box click Driver

2. Click the Roll Back Driver button

3. Follow the instructions

Read the Instructions

Computer software is much the same as a piece of machinery in that it is designed to work within a specified set of parameters. In order to reach those parameters it needs a certain level of resources. Without them it just won't work properly, if at all.

Program Requirements

The main resources that a computer program needs are processor power (CPU speed) and memory (RAM).

Before you even buy a program therefore, study the packaging and somewhere you'll see the manufacturer's recommended minimum system requirements. If your system doesn't match these, put it back on the shelf, you'll just be wasting money otherwise. Windows XP is a very good example of this and many people are blithely buying it on the assumption that it will work because their previous versions did. Unfortunately, in many cases they are finding out differently.

"Readme" Files

Somewhere, on virtually any program's installation disk, there will be a Notepad, Internet Explorer or Word document detailing system requirements as mentioned above. In addition to this however, there will also be a "Readme" or "Setup" file which will give installation and setting up instructions. You may also find a section devoted to known compatibility issues or "bugs" as they are called. This will give details of hardware devices which might not work with the program. Do read these files as they can save a lot of head scratching.

Many program installation disks, in addition to the main program, will also contain other applications which require separate installation. Some can be very useful programs in their own right and are well worth installing.

A good example of this is the TweakUI program which is in the PowerToys folder on the Windows 98 CD. This program allows the user to make many adjustments to system settings which would otherwise be impossible without a detailed knowledge of the registry. Another example is TV tuner cards which often contain video editing programs not installed by default.

So, dig out all those installation disks and have a look inside them. You will be surprised at what you find.

A Readme file on the XP installation CD. Have you read it?

Don't Lose Your Old Files & Settings

Computers are rapidly evolving machines and very quickly become, if not exactly obsolete, certainly out of date. Although they can be upgraded, eventually many people will buy a new machine.

It is possible to transfer settings and data by using third-party utilities such as Norton Ghost which is supplied as part of System Works. Ghost will make a mirror image of your hard drive and save it to a backup medium.

The problem with this of course is that when you throw away that old computer, you will also be throwing away all your data and settings. Keeping your data is not so much of a problem, as with a suitable backup medium such as Zip disks, you can make a copy and then transfer it to your new PC.

Your system settings, however, are a different matter. These will include such things as Internet/email settings, display settings, Taskbar configuration and so on. Previously, all these settings would have to be manually re-entered in the new computer – a time-consuming process.

XP provides a much easier method in the form of its new Files and Settings Transfer Wizard. However, in order to use it you will need a transfer medium such as a network or direct cable connection. Alternatively, a high-capacity drive medium such as Zip disks can be used.

If you don't possess a backup medium of suitable capacity but can establish a network connection to your new PC, you can use this method to transfer your files and settings.

Use the Wizard as follows:

1 Insert the XP installation disk in the CD-ROM drive of the old PC and when it runs, select Perform Additional tasks from the menu

2 In the new window, select Transfer Files and Settings

3 The wizard will now open. On the Welcome screen, click Next

4 Now you are asked which computer you are working on – the new one or the old one. Select the Old PC option and click next

5 A new window opens and asks you to choose a transfer method. This can be a network or direct cable connection or removable media such as Zip disks. Having made a choice, click Next

6 In the next window, you are able to choose what you want to transfer – files, settings or both. The wizard will make some suggestions in the form of a list which you can ignore if you wish

Don't even try to transfer files by using floppy disks as the medium. They simply do not have the capacity. However, they will be quite adequate for transferring system settings which should fit on one disk, two at most.

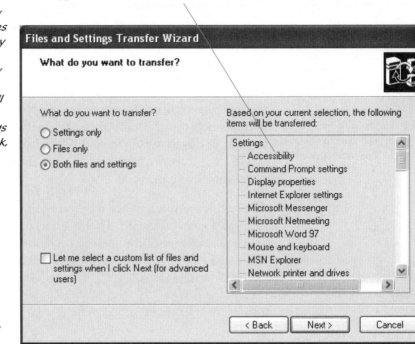

Files and Settings Transfer Wizard

What do you want to transfer?

What do you want to transfer?

○ Settings only
○ Files only
◉ Both files and settings

Based on your current selection, the following items will be transferred:

Settings
 Accessibility
 Command Prompt settings
 Display properties
 Internet Explorer settings
 Microsoft Messenger
 Microsoft Netmeeting
 Microsoft Word 97
 Mouse and keyboard
 MSN Explorer
 Network printer and drives

☐ Let me select a custom list of files and settings when I click Next (for advanced users)

[< Back] [Next >] [Cancel]

The Files and Settings Transfer Wizard allows you to move settings and files from PCs running Windows 9x, ME, 2000, NT4.0 and XP.

7 The Wizard will now save the settings and/or files you have chosen

8 A message appears telling you that this part of the procedure is finished and that you must now go to the new computer

9 At the new PC, run the Wizard again

10 When you see the "Which Computer is this" window, select New Computer

11 In the next window, enter the location from which the files are coming and then click Next. Now the files will be transferred. When the procedure is finished, click Finish

Running Older Applications On XP

If applications which worked OK with your previous version of Windows refuse to do so with XP, don't chuck them out before trying XP's Program Compatibility Wizard.

It is universally recognized that XP Home Edition is in many ways, a vast improvement on its predecessors, system stability being one obvious example. This is due to the fact that its basic architecture is based on NT, the professional version of Windows. However, NT was not designed for the home environment and has never been suitable for certain applications, games being just one example.

With XP Home Edition, Microsoft have attempted to take the best features from both its home environment and professional systems and combine them into one "super" system.

Unfortunately, it has to be said that they haven't got it quite right yet and one example of this is the fact that some applications that worked fine on the previous versions will not do so on XP.

Microsoft have recognized this problem and to help alleviate it have included a Program Compatibility Wizard with XP. The application works by attempting to create an environment in which a particular program will work, i.e. Windows 95, 98 or ME and is accessible from Start, All Programs, Accessories.

The Program Compatibility Wizard works by "fooling" the program into thinking it is running on the previous Windows version.

Use it as follows:

1 Access the Wizard as described above. The Help and Support Center, which houses the wizard, opens. Click Next

2 Choose the program you want to run in Compatibility Mode. You can choose from a list or locate it yourself manually

3 The Compatibility Mode window now appears as shown on the following page

A quick way to open a program in Compatibility mode is to right click it, select Properties and then click the Compatibility tab.

...cont'd

Although Program Compatibility works well in most cases, it can require a few tweaks and adjustments before it gets things right. You may have to exercise a little bit of patience.

Help and Support Center

Search ☐ →
Set search options

Help and Support Center
Windows XP Home Edition

Program Compatibility Wizard

Select a compatibility mode for the program

Choose the operating system that is recommended for this program, or that previously supported the program correctly:

○ Microsoft Windows 95

○ Microsoft Windows NT 4.0 (Service Pack 5)

○ Microsoft Windows 98 / Windows Me

○ Microsoft Windows 2000

◉ Do not apply a compatibility mode

[< Back] [Next >] [Cancel]

4 Choose the operating system you want to emulate

Once the Wizard has successfully set up a program, the settings will be retained. Every time the program is run, the settings will be applied.

5 A Display Settings window now appears. Choose any display setting restrictions you may need and then click Next

6 You will now see a summary of your selections. Test them by clicking Next

7 The specified program will now open and XP applies the compatibility settings. Use the program and make sure it is working as it should. If it is, click Yes and then Next. In the new window select Yes, set this program to always use these compatibility settings

8 If the program doesn't work, select No and try different settings

9 Once you have accepted the compatibility settings for a program, every time it's run, it will use those settings

Disk Management With XP

You may find that the Disk Management option is not available from Computer Management. In this case go back to Control Panel and click Performance. Then from the File menu click Add/Remove Snap-in. In the next window click Add, in the next window select Disk Management and Add. Then select This Computer in the final Window. Go back to Computer Management and Disk management will now be available.

Disk management is basically the process whereby hard drives can be formatted and split into partitions which appear to the system as individual drives. This is a complicated issue which is beyond the scope of this book to adequately address and should only be attempted by users who know what they are doing.

The ability to do this is not specific to XP, users of ME and earlier can also carry out disk management. The difference with XP is that it is now possible to do it via a Windows interface rather than a DOS interface. This makes it a much more intuitive and a faster process. Access XP's disk management utility as described below:

1 Go to Start. Control Panel and Administrative Tools

2 Click Computer Management and then click Disk Management

This utility is not for beginners. Improper use can wipe your drives clean and render your system unusable. Bone up on the subject first.

You will find that many of the options are not actually available with the Home edition of XP. To make full use of Disk Management you will need to run XP Professional.

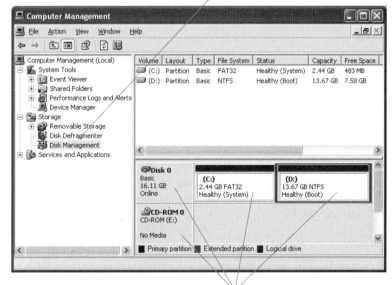

3 The right-hand window shows what disks, partitions, etc. are installed on the PC

4 Right clicking on the drives in the lower right-hand window shows what options are available

What File System To Use?

Unlike previous versions of Windows, XP gives the user a choice of file systems – FAT and NTFS.

The first – FAT, is the one found on ME and earlier and is the system XP installs by default. This is mainly because of backward compatibility as only XP and Windows 2000 will be able to read files on a NTFS partition or drive. The point here is that if the user is planning to use XP's dual boot facility to switch between XP and earlier versions, they should use FAT otherwise they will not be able to access the NTFS partition or drive with an earlier Windows version. This is the only real advantage in staying with FAT.

If the above is not an issue for you then NTFS is the system to install. One of the major reasons for this is the security features it provides. Whereas FAT limits you to basic share and user-level security, NTFS allows much greater levels of security with both the operating system itself and also on networks. For example, NTFS allows individual files or folders to be securely encrypted.

NTFS also makes drive and folder compression much easier than previous versions. This is done by right clicking the drive or folder, selecting Properties and then the Compress option.

NTFS is a much more robust file system and unlike FAT, where it is advisable to run Scandisk or a similar disk checking utility on a regular basis, will rarely require this to be done.

The option to convert your drive to a dynamic drive is only available with XP Pro.

For the more advanced user, NTFS offers a whole host of extra features amongst which is the concept of *dynamic drives* which can be roughly equated to a partition on an ordinary drive. XP allows the user to convert an ordinary drive into a dynamic drive. The advantages of this are safety and flexibility. For example, data can be easily duplicated on two seperate drives so that if one fails the data isn't lost.

Shortcuts

One of the best ways to increase the efficiency with which you use your PC is by means of shortcuts. This chapter shows you how to create some of these useful items.

Covers

Chapter Nine

Add Pop-Up Menus to the Taskbar

This is a useful way of creating a shortcut to your favorite applications or files. It is also very simple to do by following the instructions below:

1 Create a folder on your desktop and give it a suitable name

2 Now simply drag and drop shortcuts to the desired applications to this folder

3 Click the folder and drag it to the right-hand side of the Taskbar

4 Now you will see your folder on the Taskbar with a double chevron to its right. Click this and a pop-up menu will appear displaying the contents of the folder

Good organization is a major factor when it comes to getting a job done quickly and efficiently. This applies to any task. If you're constantly having to hunt about for your tools, it's surprising how much time this can waste.
The tip on this page will enable you to get a job done on your computer with the minimum of fuss.

A practical method of utilizing this tip is to create a pop-up menu containing shortcuts to all the applications you need for a particular task. For example, if you happen to be writing a book, you can have instantly at hand all the tools you need. This saves constantly opening, closing and reopening related files, folders and programs. The illustration below is an example of this:

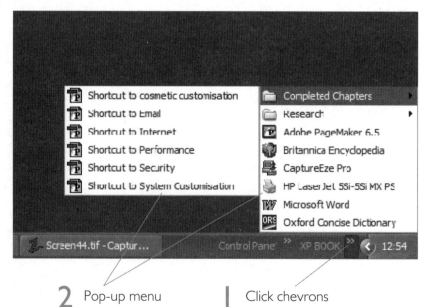

2 Pop-up menu | Click chevrons

Create Hotkey Shortcuts

There will be occasions when you want to open a program in a hurry but don't wish to close the current window so that you can get to it.

You could always click the Show Desktop icon on the Taskbar but you've still got to navigate your way to wherever the program or file is located.

There is however, a much quicker way and this involves utilizing your keyboard.

You can create a lot of shortcuts in this way, so many in fact, that you might well have difficulty in remembering them all.

Write them down on a piece of paper and stick it on the wall near the monitor.

1 Create a Desktop shortcut to the program by right clicking it and selecting Send To, Desktop (create shortcut)

2 Right click the shortcut on the desktop and select Properties. The following dialog box will open:

Microsoft Word Properties

General | Shortcut | Compatibility

Microsoft Word

Target type: Application
Target location: Office
Target: Files\Microsoft Office\Office\WINWORD.EXE"

Start in:
Shortcut key: None
Run: Normal window
Comment:

Find Target... | Change Icon... | Advanced...

OK | Cancel | Apply

3 Click the Shortcut key entry which is currently reading None

4 Now simply hit the key on the keyboard you wish to use as the shortcut key e.g. "W"

5 The Shortcut key box will now read:

CTRL+ALT+W

6 Click OK and from now on you can instantly open the application by pressing CTRL+ALT+W simultaneously

Use the Windows Logo Key

Situated on modern keyboards between the Ctrl and Alt keys is a key with a logo of a flying window on it. This is the Windows logo key and with it you can quickly open a number of applications on your computer.

 The Windows logo key shortcuts can be surprisingly useful in certain situations. Don't ignore them.

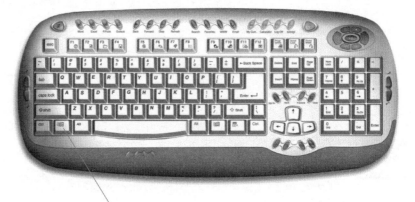

Windows Logo Key

Useful commands:

WINDOWS	Display the Start menu.
WINDOWS+D	Minimize or restore all windows.
WINDOWS+E	Display Windows Explorer.
WINDOWS+F	Display Windows's Search utility.
WINDOWS+R	Display Run dialog box.
WINDOWS+BREAK	Display the System Properties dialog box.
WINDOWS+SHIFT+M	Undo minimize all windows.
WINDOWS+U	Open Utility Manager.
WINDOWS+L	Lock Computer.

Do a Quick Keyword Search

This technique can also be used with other Windows text applications such as Notepad and WordPad. It can also be very useful when carrying out searches on the Internet. Some Web pages can be extremely long and if you are looking for a particular topic and find yourself wading through reams of unrelated stuff, using Ctrl+F can be a real time saver.

The ability to carry out almost instantaneous searches is an extremely useful and often overlooked feature of computers.

For example, by using Windows Search application, it is possible to carry out an entire search of a computer's contents for literally anything. To do this though, it is necessary to set up various search parameters and thus it really couldn't be described as quick.

However, Windows does provide another, more basic, search tool which can be used for carrying out quick searches in text-based applications such as word processors and Web pages.

Let's say for example, that you have open a lengthy Web page and are looking for all instances of a specific word but have neither the time nor inclination to read through the whole page.

What you need to do is press Ctrl+F on your keyboard which will open the Find dialog box as shown below:

Type the word you wish to find in the Find what box

Find	? X

Find what: |

☐ Match whole word only
☐ Match case

Direction
○ Up ◉ Down

Find Next

Cancel

2 To find further instances, click the Find Next button

This tip will work in all Windows text applications.

Automatically Delete Files

The Recycle Bin is provided by Windows as a safety measure to prevent people deleting stuff by accident and to also give them a second chance should they have a rethink.

Exercise caution when automatically deleting files as it's all too easy to simply make a mistake and delete the wrong file. Remember, if you do, you will not be able to get it back. Although XP will not allow you to delete essential system files, it will quite happily trash your data files such as Word documents.

However, unless the Recycle Bin is cleared out periodically, the data it contains can mount up to sizable proportions.

To prevent this there is a way to bypass it completely although this means that once deleted, a file is gone for good.

This can be set up as follows:

1   Right click the Recycle Bin and select Properties

There are third-party utility programs on the market which can retrieve or "undelete" mistakenly deleted files. Examples are Norton System Works and Nuts & Bolts. Programs of this type also offer a whole host of other useful tools.

Recycle Bin Properties

Global | Local Disk (C:) | Local Disk (D:)

○ Configure drives independently
● Use one setting for all drives:

☐ Do not move files to the Recycle Bin.
Remove files immediately when deleted

10%

Maximum size of Recycle Bin (percent of each drive)

☑ Display delete confirmation dialog

OK   Cancel   Apply

2   Check the box which reads Do not move files to the Recycle Bin.

Another way to bypass the Recycle Bin, is to simply hold down the Shift key as you click Delete.

3   You can also prevent a confirmation message from appearing each time you delete a file, by unchecking this

4   From now on, whenever you delete a file, that's it. It's gone for good. Just be careful if you decide to select this option

Quick Access to Device Manager

Windows' Device Manager is one of the most important tools available to a computer owner. It gives him or her access to all the hardware on the PC and allows changes to be made to their configuration and settings. It will also give visual warnings in the form of coded symbols, when something has gone wrong. Not only this, it can even suggest a suitable course of action to remedy the fault.

The Device Manager is hidden away in the Control Panel under Systems, Hardware and is not too easily accessible. A good way of creating instant Desktop access is as follows:

One of the biggest problems users experience with XP is its reluctance to accept older hardware. However, many of these problems can be resolved by updating the relevant device drivers. Device Manager is the place to do it.

1 Right click the Desktop and select New, Shortcut

2 In the box, type the following exactly as it reads, including spaces:

%windir%\system32\mmc.exe %windir%\system32\devmgmt.msc

Device Manager is the place to look when any of your system devices stop working or are not working as they should. It will often be able to tell you the nature of the problem and what to do about it.

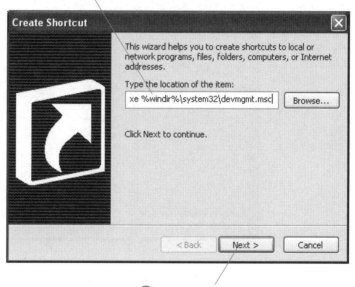

Create Shortcut

This wizard helps you to create shortcuts to local or network programs, files, folders, computers, or Internet addresses.

Type the location of the item:

xe %windir%\system32\devmgmt.msc   Browse...

Click Next to continue.

< Back   Next >   Cancel

Device Manager is also a useful source of information about your system resources.

3 Click Next and in the next dialog box give your shortcut a suitable name

4 A new icon will appear on the Desktop

5 Clicking the icon will take you directly to the Device Manager

Instant Screensavers

Before you can set up an instant screensaver, you first need to find its location in the Windows folder. You can do this as follows:

1 Go to the Windows folder on the hard drive, open it and locate a folder called "System32"

2 Inside the System32 folder, you'll see some little monitor-shaped icons (you'll have to scroll down to find them). These will be prefaced with the letters "ss" and are the screensavers installed on your system

To configure the settings for your screensaver shortcuts, simply right click and choose from the available options.

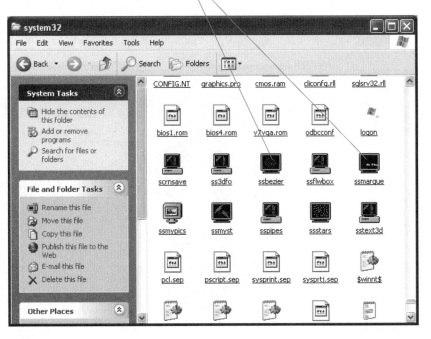

3 Right click the ones you want and then select Send To, Desktop (create shortcut)

4 Back on the Desktop, to activate your screensaver, all you have to do is click on it

Windows Keyboard Shortcuts

General Keyboard Shortcuts:

 Many people use their keyboard almost exclusively for typing text into various applications and their mouse for opening and closing programs, saving and deleting, etc.

While there is absolutely nothing wrong with this, they are missing out on what is often a quicker way to do many of these actions. Most of the things you can do with a mouse can also be done with a keyboard.

CTRL+C	Copy.
CTRL+X	Cut.
CTRL+V	Paste.
CTRL+Z	Undo.
DELETE	Delete.
SHIFT+DELETE	Delete an item permanently.
CTRL while dragging	Copy the selected item.
CTRL+SHIFT while dragging	Creates a shortcut to the selected item.
F2	Rename the selected item.
CTRL+A	Select all.
F3	Search for a file or a folder.
ALT+ENTER	View the properties for the selected item.
ALT+F4	Close the active item or the active program.
ALT+ENTER	Display the properties of the selected object.
ALT+SPACEBAR	Open the shortcut menu for the active window.
CTRL+F4	Close the active document.
ALT+TAB	Switch between the open items.
ALT+ESC	Cycle through items in the order opened.
F6	Cycle through screen elements.
F4	Display the Address bar list in My Computer or Windows Explorer.
SHIFT+F10	Display the selected item's shortcut menu.
ALT+SPACEBAR	Display the System menu for the active window.
CTRL+ESC	Display the Start menu.
ALT+Underlined letter in a menu name	Display the corresponding menu.
F10	Activate the menu bar in the active program.
RIGHT ARROW	Open the next menu to the right or a submenu.
LEFT ARROW	Open the next menu to the left.

F5	Update the active window.
BACKSPACE	View the folder one level up in My Computer or Windows Explorer.
ESC	Cancel the current task.
SHIFT when inserting a CD	Prevent the CD from automatically playing.

If you find using a mouse difficult for any reason, give the little creature a rest and take to your keyboard. You'll be surprised at what you can achieve with it.

Dialog Box Keyboard Shortcuts:

CTRL+TAB	Move forward through the tabs.
CTRL+SHIFT+TAB	Move backward through the tabs.
TAB	Move forward through the options.
SHIFT+TAB	Move backward through the options.
ALT+Underlined letter	Perform/select a command or option.
ENTER	Perform the command for the active option or button.
SPACEBAR	Select or clear the active check box.
ARROW KEYS	Select a button if the active option is a group of option buttons.
F1	Display Help.
F4	Display the items in the active list.
BACKSPACE	Open a folder one level up if a folder is selected in the Save As or Open dialog box.

Mice are mechanical devices and as such are as prone to failure as any other device. If you know how to use your keyboard, it will provide a useful backup to your mouse should it ever die on you.

Accessibility Keyboard Shortcuts:

RIGHT SHIFT (8 seconds)	Switch FilterKeys on or off.
LEFT ALT+LEFT SHIFT+PRINT SCREEN	Switch High Contrast on or off.
LEFT ALT+LEFT SHIFT+NUM LOCK	Switch MouseKeys on or off.
SHIFT 5 times	Switch the StickyKeys either on or off.
NUM LOCK (5 seconds)	Switch the ToggleKeys on or off.
WINDOWS LOGO+U	Open Utility Manager.

Miscellaneous

There are many computer tips which are difficult to assign to a particular category. So we have put them here.

Covers

Chapter Ten

Stop XP Asking For the Installation Disk

Most people will at some time or other be in the process of installing an application only to suddenly see a message pop up asking them to insert the Windows CD in the CD-ROM drive:

The i386 folder is some 486MB in size. If you don't have too much hard drive space to start with, then maybe you should think twice before using this tip.

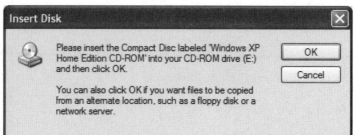

This happens because, for the application in question to work, certain files have to be copied from the Windows installation disk.

To prevent this happening, do the following:

1 Place the Windows installation CD into the CD-ROM drive. Go to My Computer, right click the CD-ROM drive icon and then click Open. This will reveal the contents of the CD

2 Find the folder called i386, right click and select Copy. Now go to your hard drive, right click an empty area and click Paste. The i386 folder will now be copied to the hard drive

When it needs certain files, XP will, by default, go to the CD-ROM drive and look for the installation CD. By amending the registry, we are telling it to look elsewhere (the i386 folder on your hard drive).

Now you need to edit the Registry so that the system can find the files you have just transferred to your hard drive:

1 Open the Registry by typing "regedit" in Run in the Start menu

2 By clicking on the + signs, expand the Registry and locate the following entry:

HKEY_LOCAL_MACHINE\Software\Microsoft\WindowsNT\ CurrentVersion

3 Click the CurrentVersion folder

The Registry Editor has a search function called Find. This is available from Edit on the menu bar. This facility can be useful if you know what you are looking for.

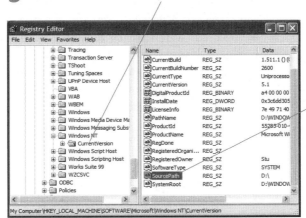

4 Double-click SourcePath

5 In the Value Data box alter the current entry to read C:\i386 (C being your hard drive). Click OK

6 Now find the registry entry at:

HKEY_LOCAL_MACHINE\Software\Microsoft\Windows\CurrentVersion\Setup

7 Click the Setup folder and then double click SourcePath

When you have completed step 8, reboot the PC and from now on you will never be asked for the installation disk again.

8 In the Edit string dialog box, change the current setting to read C:\

Keyboard Mouse

The 2 and 8 keys will move the cursor up and down, the 4 and 6 keys left and right and the 7,3,1 and 9 keys will move it diagonally. The 5 key will open a highlighted option. Holding the Ctrl key down will speed up the cursor while the Shift key will slow it down.

It's not unknown for a mouse to suddenly stop working for some reason – its connection to the PC may have been knocked loose, there may be a problem with its driver or the mouse itself may have failed. When any of these scenarios occur you'll find you are unable to control your PC. This can be serious if you are in the middle of a long project and haven't saved it yet. Without the mouse how will you be able to get to the Save button? You stand a real chance of losing all your work. If this should happen to you try doing the following:

1. First activate your mouse keys by holding down the left Alt and Shift keys on your keyboard simultaneously. Then press the Num Lock key

2. You'll find you are now able to control the cursor by using the numerical keypad on the right of the keyboard

You now have two options:

1. Use the mouse keys to access File, Save/Save As from the menu bar. This can be a tricky performance

2. A better option is to simply press Ctrl+S on the keyboard. This will open the program's Save dialog box. Now you can use the mouse keys to move the cursor to the Save button

Pressing Ctrl+S will open the Save As dialog box in Windows applications such as WordPad, Notepad and Word. It may not work in third-party programs. If this is the case you will have to access the Save As dialog box from the program's File menu on the menu bar.

Having saved your work you now need to switch the computer off so that you can investigate the mouse fault. Do this by pressing the Windows key on the keyboard and then by using the arrow keys, highlight the Turn Off Computer button and then hit Enter and then Turn Off or Restart.

Now all you have to do is find out what's up with the mouse.

Keyboard Calculator

Here is a handy shortcut which allows you to operate XP's calculator without having to bother with the mouse.

1 Open XP's calculator by going to Start, All Programs, Accessories, Calculator (you can also type "calc" in the Run application available from the Start Menu)

Don't forget that XP's calculator can be expanded to a scientific calculator. This option is available from the Menu Bar under View.

While the calculator supplied by Windows is perfectly adequate for most needs, there is a whole range of far superior and specialized calculators available for download from the Internet.

2 Instead of fiddling about with the mouse to activate the keys, simply use the numeric keypad on the keyboard:

/ key	The equivalent of divide.
* key	The equivalent of multipy.
+ key	The equivalent of add.
- key	The equivalent of subtract.
Enter	The equivalent of =.

Successful Minesweeping

Here is another tip for those of you who always like to win and which will enable you to amaze your friends.

1   Open a new game of Minesweeper

2   Click anywhere on the title bar and then type "xyzzy" on your keyboard. Press Shift and Enter

3   At the top left-hand corner of the desktop you will now see a single white pixel (you'll have to look hard to see it)

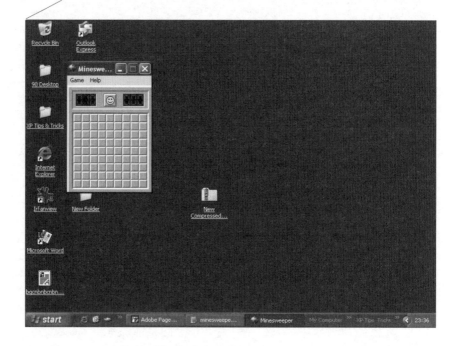

4   As you move the mouse cursor over the game blocks, the pixel will disappear when placed over a block containing a bomb. That's all there is to it

Force a Win At Freecell

This is a useless tip if ever there was one but someone somewhere might appreciate it.

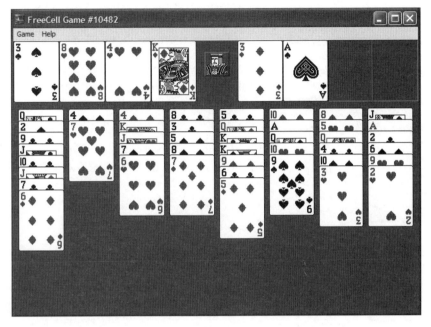

This tip doesn't work with other games such as Solitaire and Spider. So, don't even bother trying.

| All you have to do is press Ctrl+Shift+F10 on the keyboard. Then you'll see the following:

User-Friendly User Interface

? Choose Abort to Win,
Retry to Lose,
or Ignore to Cancel.

Abort   Retry   Ignore

2 Click Abort and you're a winner

Compress Files and Folders With XP

Another way to use XP's compression feature is by simply right clicking the desktop and selecting New, Compressed (zipped) folder. This will create an empty zipped folder. To use it simply drag your files and drop them in the folder where they will be automatically compressed.

Any third-party compression programs may also have entries here:

A very useful way of employing file compression is the creation of backup folders of important data. Ideally, these would be placed on a separate drive. Alternatively, you can use compression to store little-used files that you might otherwise delete in order to reclaim the disk space.

Compression is most effective in terms of reducing file size when employed with text-based files and can achieve compression rates of 50% or more. Graphics files, on the other hand, might only be reduced by about 10%.

Many people like to keep their hard drive as free as possible and one way to achieve this is by what's known as file compression.

To compress a file or folder you need a special compression program which will not only compress the file but will also decompress it when it's needed.

There are several of these on the market, the most popular being WinZip, a program which is commonly available from PC magazine cover CDs. However, being a third-party utility, you need to physically install it on your PC.

Unlike previous versions of Windows, XP comes with a built in file compression utility of its own. To use it do the following:

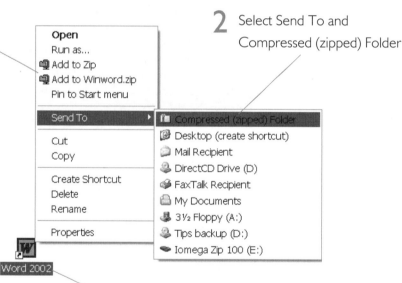

2 Select Send To and Compressed (zipped) Folder

1 Right click the file to be compressed

3 Your file will now be copied, compressed and placed in a zipped folder. The original file will still be available in its uncompressed state

XP's Icon Folders

XP comes with hundreds of system icons which are hidden away in files with the .dll extension. To search through them all would be a mammoth task, so we will show you how to access the two main icon folders.

There are literally thousands of icons, covering every conceivable topic, freely available for download from the Internet.

Go to any search engine and try typing "Computer Icons" in the search box. You won't know where to start.

1 Right click any shortcut and then click Properties

2 In the new window, on the Shortcut tab click Change Icon

3 In the box type:

C:\WINDOWS\System32\ pifmrg.dll

Then click OK

4 Resulting list of icons

For those of you who still hanker after Windows' old icons, some of them are available in the icon list produced by Step 5.

5 Alternatively, in step 3 type:

%SystemRoot%\system32\SHELL32.DLL

Then click OK for even more icons

Silence the Modem

Essential things though they may be, modems have an irritating way of announcing themselves when activated. This manifests itself in the form of what can be best described as a series of strangulated buzzes, clicks and whirrs.

This tip only applies to those of you with an internal modem. If you have an external model then you should be able to turn down the volume manually.

If you are one of those types with strange nocturnal habits such as browsing the Internet when normal people are tucked up in bed, it can also be a nuisance.

So, you'll be glad to know that there is a way to shut it up.

You can do it as follows:

1 Go to Start, Control Panel, Phone and Modem Options

2 Click Modems, Properties, Modem. This opens the following dialog box:

3 Under Speaker volume, drag the slider to the Off position

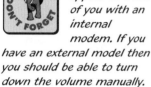

XP's On-Screen Keyboard

This is a handy tip for those who have difficulty using a keyboard due to a physical disability, for example. Alternatively, your keyboard may have simply packed up. If you were running previous versions of Windows you would have little option but to stop using the PC until such time as you could get the keyboard repaired or replaced.

Windows XP, however, comes galloping to the rescue with its on-screen keyboard. This can be accessed as follows:

The on-screen keyboard is obviously much slower than a normal keyboard but in an emergency could be a godsend.

1. Go to Start, All Programs, Accessories, Accessibility. When you open the application you will see the following:

2. From Keyboard on the menu bar you can open an Enhanced version which will provide additional keys (the numerical keypad)

Enhanced keyboard:

Batch Renaming of Files

Have you ever been in a situation whereby you have a whole load of related files with an assortment of meaningless or unrelated names? To make order of them you have to individually rename each file which is a laborious task.

With XP, all that is now a thing of the past. It provides you with a means of sequentially renaming any number of files with minimum effort. You can do it as described below:

1 Open the folder containing the files to be renamed

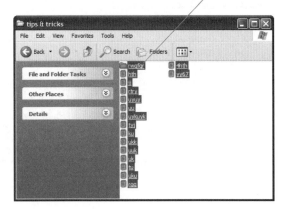

2 From the Edit menu on the Menu bar, click Select All. All the files will now be highlighted as shown below:

...cont'd

tips & tricks

File   Edit   View   Favorites   Tools   Help

Back   •   Search   Folders

File and Folder Tasks

Other Places

Details

Photo's
4hth
hth   yy67
ji
rtry
uyuy
uu
uykuyk
tyi
ku
ukk
uuk
uk
tu
uku
rqq

If you only want to rename some of the files in a folder then use your mouse to select the ones you want and then rename the first selected file.

3   Right click the first file in the list and select Rename. Type a suitable name and then click once anywhere in the folder. The files will now be automatically renamed

If for any reason you want to revert to the original file names, you can go to Undo in the Edit menu. This option however, will only allow you to "undo" a maximum of 10 files.

tips & tricks

File   Edit   View   Favorites   Tools   Help

Back   •   Search   Folders

File and Folder Tasks

Other Places

Details

Photo's
Photo's (15)
Photo's (1)   Photo's (16)
Photo's (2)
Photo's (3)
Photo's (4)
Photo's (5)
Photo's (6)
Photo's (7)
Photo's (8)
Photo's (9)
Photo's (10)
Photo's (11)
Photo's (12)
Photo's (13)
Photo's (14)

Get Media Player 2 Back

The media player bundled with Windows XP is a radical departure from the classic Media Player 2 which was a stalwart of older versions of Windows. It has a much busier interface and a whole range of new features. Regardless of all that however, it still doesn't play movies as smoothly as Media Player 2 does. Plus it takes longer to open a media file.

Many people also prefer the slick and uncomplicated interface of Media Player 2.

While Media Player 2 is still available on XP, Microsoft have seen fit to hide it away. However, you can get it back as follows:

If you want the look of Media Player 2 whilst retaining all the new features of XP's player, you can apply a Media Player 2 "skin" from the Skin Chooser tab.
There are also a whole range of other skins from which to choose.

1 Go to Start, Run and in the box, type "mplayer2". It will now open. To make it the default player, go to steps 2 and 3 below

While Media Player 2 may have the edge on performance, Windows Media Player provides a whole range of options that the older player doesn't. For example, you can change brightness and contrast with Windows Media Player which can make a poor quality movie watchable.

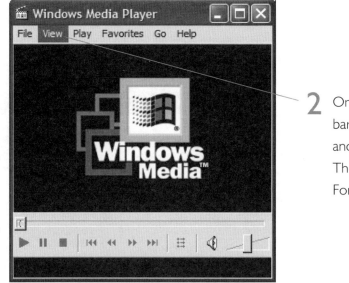

2 On the menu bar select View and Options. Then click the Formats tab

3 Choose the file formats you want to open with Media Player 2 by checking the appropriate checkboxes

4 All the selected formats will now open with the classic player

Locate XP's Backup Program

Previous versions of Windows have all come with an inbuilt backup utility, as does XP Professional. Try looking for one in XP Home Edition, though, and you won't find it. This is for the simple reason that it just isn't there.

XP's Backup program and Files and Settings Transfer Wizard will provide the user with all the facilities needed to make complete or partial backups of the system.

However, you may remember that in a previous tip, it was recommended that you make a point of examining the contents of installation disks because of the chance of unearthing some goodies that aren't installed by default.

Well, XP's backup utility proves the point.

1 Place the XP installation disk in the CD-ROM drive and then go to My Computer. Right click the drive and then click Open. This will display the contents of the CD as shown below:

2 Click the VALUEADD folder

To make use of any backup application, you will need a storage medium. Writable CDs are a good option. However, with the low cost of hard drives these days, it makes good sense to install a second hard drive. This can then be used to make a "mirror" image of your existing drive.

3 Click the MSFT folder and then the NTBACKUP folder

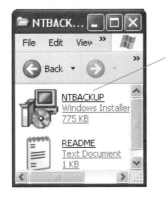

4 Now you will see the Backup program's Setup file. Just click to execute it. XP's Backup application will now be available from Start, All Programs, Accessories, System Tools

Where Did ScanDisk Go?

Users more familiar with the old Windows interface may be wondering what happened to ScanDisk, the disk error checking tool. The answer is that it's still alive and well in XP, although it's now masquerading under the new name of Checkdisk (chkdsk).

 Checkdisk is not available from System Tools under All Programs, Accessories, as it was with Windows ME and prior versions. To access it in XP, right click the drive and go to Properties, Tools.

You can access it as follows:

1 In My Computer, right click any drive and then select Properties

2 In the next window click Tools

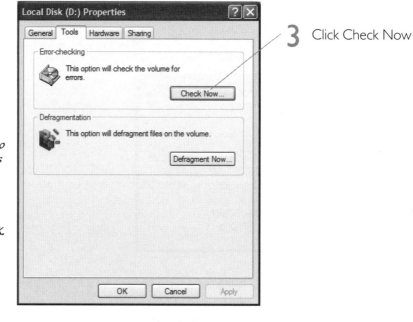

3 Click Check Now

 Another way to open Chkdsk is from a command prompt. Go to Start, Run and in the box type "chkdsk". Then click OK.

4 Choose from the available options and then click Start

Be On Time With XP

The clock in your computer is powered in exactly the same way as the majority of clocks and watches are these days – batteries.

For automatic synchronization to work effectively, you will need a permanent Internet connection such as cable or DSL.

The batteries used in computers are usually of a high quality and will keep good time over a period of two to three years. Eventually, however, they will begin to degrade and the clock will start to lose time. While it's no big deal to reset it, XP has made it even easier with its Internet Time Synchronization feature.

This little gem is hidden away in the depths of the Control Panel in the Date and Time applet.

| Open Date and Time and then click the Internet Time tab

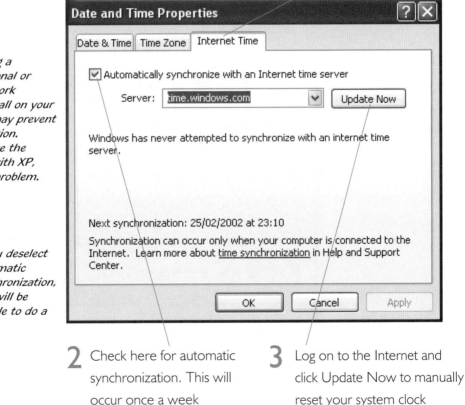

Using a personal or network firewall on your PC may prevent clock synchronization. However, if you use the firewall bundled with XP, there won't be a problem.

If you deselect automatic synchronization, you will be unable to do a manual update.

2 Check here for automatic synchronization. This will occur once a week

3 Log on to the Internet and click Update Now to manually reset your system clock

Listen To XP

Windows XP has a new feature which is designed to provide assistance to the visually impaired.

This is called Narrator and is a simple text to speech utility. Narrator will read aloud what is displayed on your screen – the contents of the active window, menu options, or any text that you have typed.

XP's Narrator is designed to work with specific Windows applications. It might also work with others but the results aren't guaranteed.

The application is designed to work with Notepad, WordPad, Control Panel programs, Internet Explorer, Windows Desktop, and Windows setup. If you attempt to use it with other programs, it may read the words incorrectly.

You can access Narrator by going to Start, All Programs, Accessories, Accessibility, Narrator. When you open the program you will see that you are provided with several options as shown in the illustration below.

If you use Narrator, keep it minimized on the Taskbar. There is no need to have its window open.

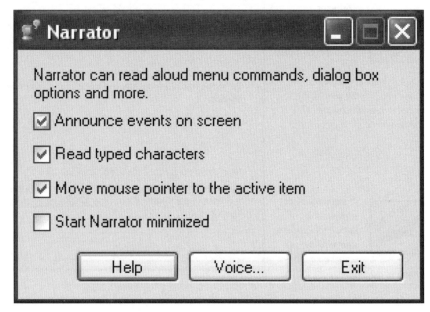

Narrator

Narrator can read aloud menu commands, dialog box options and more.

☑ Announce events on screen

☑ Read typed characters

☑ Move mouse pointer to the active item

☐ Start Narrator minimized

[Help]   [Voice...]   [Exit]

The program can also be opened by opening Run on the Start Menu and typing Narrator in the box.

This program will prove to be invaluable to many people.

XP's Visual Warnings

XP has a system for generating visual warnings, a feature which can be useful for the hard of hearing.

The application allows the user to select from several types of visual warning when the system makes a sound.

To configure this do the following:

1 Go to Start, Control Panel, Accessibility Options and select the Sound tab

Accessibility Options [?][X]

Keyboard | Sound | Display | Mouse | General

SoundSentry

Use SoundSentry if you want Windows to generate visual warnings when your system makes a sound.

[✓] Use SoundSentry

Choose the visual warning:

Flash active caption bar ▼

[None]
Flash active caption bar
Flash active window
Flash desktop

the speech and sounds they make.

[✓] Use ShowSounds

[OK] [Cancel] [Apply]

2 You can use SoundSentry to generate visual warnings such as flashing the Desktop

3 Alternatively, ShowSounds will display captions for any speech or sounds made by the system

Create an XP Boot Disk

Reliable though XP no doubt is, it is not infallible and one day you may have the unfortunate experience of discovering that it just will not load. This situation can occur when the active partition boot record or other required files become corrupted. While there are various things that you can do in this situation, it is not possible to describe all the options here.

One thing you can do however, is to create a boot floppy disk which may enable you to get XP going in a situation as described above. Do it now though, when disaster occurs it will be to late.

1 You need to open your hard drive and locate the following files: Boot.ini, NTLDR and Ntdetect.com. Before you can do so though, you'll need to uncover them as they are by default hidden from view. Do this by opening any window and from the menu bar selecting Tools, Folder Options and then View

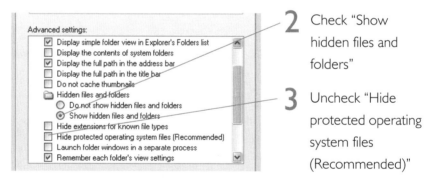

2 Check "Show hidden files and folders"

3 Uncheck "Hide protected operating system files (Recommended)"

4 Insert a floppy disk into the floppy drive. It's a good idea to format it at this stage to ensure it's in good order. Do this by right clicking the drive and selecting Format

5 Right click each of the above files in turn, select Copy and then go to the floppy disk, right click and click Paste

6 Remove the disk, label it and put it somewhere safe

Use XP's Search utility if you have trouble locating these files. Copy them directly from the Search results window to the floppy disk.

Media Content Protection

Many people use their PCs to copy music to and from CDs. This can be for their own use or to share with others. It's a popular pastime.

It is illegal to copy and distribute content that is protected by copyright.

Users who are accustomed to doing this may discover a problem when they attempt do so with XP's Media Player. This is due to a feature of this utility known as Content Protection. What this does is to prevent music files created with Media Player being copied from one computer to another.

So before you burn a load of music to a writeable CD to send to a friend, make sure Content Protection is turned off (it is enabled by default). Do it as follows:

1   On Media Player's menu bar go to Tools and then click Options

2   Click the Copy Music tab and then remove the check mark from the Protect content box as shown below:

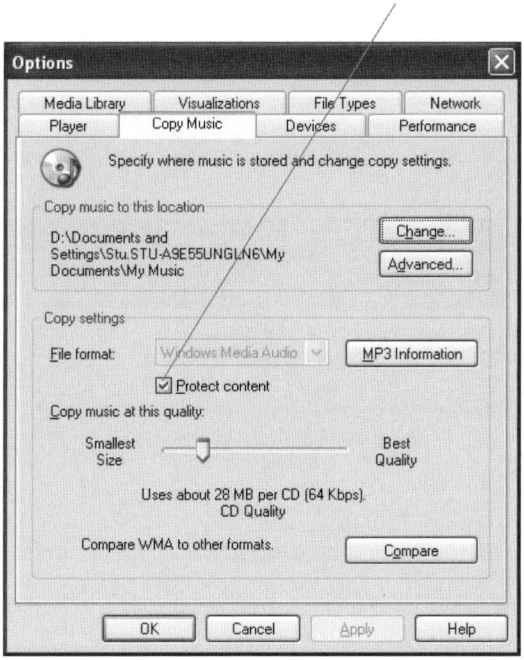

Now you will be able to make recordings that your friends will be able to play.

Windows Update Catalog

Users who like to keep their version of Windows up to date will by necessity be familiar with the Windows Update site. From here it is possible to download patches, updated versions of Microsoft applications such as Internet Explorer and drivers, etc.

The problem with this for users of ME and earlier Windows versions is that downloads obtained in this way are automatically installed for them. It isn't possible to save them as a file and then install them manually as and when required. This can be a major pain in the neck should, for example, it ever be necessary to re-format the drive and then reload Windows. The updates will be lost and thus must be downloaded again, a process which can take many hours.

XP users are spared this irritation as they have access to XP's version of Windows Update which is known as the Windows Catalog. To connect to this site do the following:

1 Logon to the Internet

2 Go to Start, All Programs and Windows Catalog

Only users of XP and Windows 2000 will be able to access the Windows Catalog site.

3 You will now be taken to the Windows Catalog site

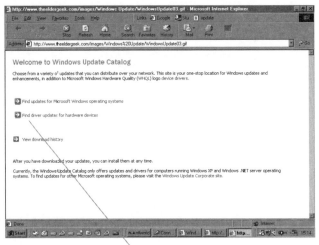

4 Choose from operating system or hardware device updates

...cont'd

Updates downloaded from the Windows Catalog site can be saved as files and thus it should never be necessary to have to download them again.

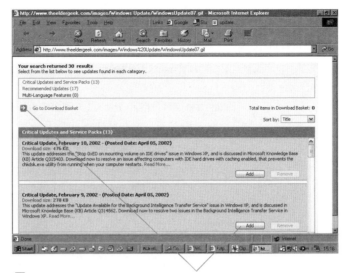

5 Choose the updates you want by clicking Add and then click "Go to Download Basket"

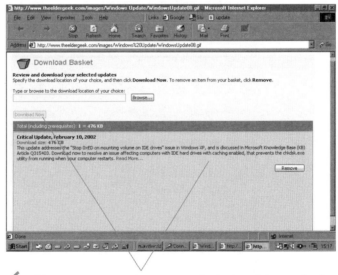

6 Now you can review your selected updates and when happy download them by clicking "Download Now"

Faxing With XP

Just one of the many new Windows features to be found on XP is the Fax console. However, it isn't installed by default so if you want to give it a try you will have to manually install it from the XP CD. Do this as follows:

1 Place the XP CD in the CD-ROM drive

2 Go to Control panel, Add or Remove Programs. At the left of the new dialog box click Add/Remove Windows Components

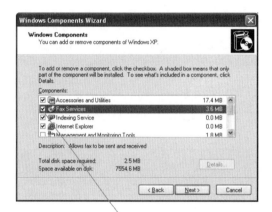

3 Check Fax Services to install the Fax Console. Access it via Start, All Programs, Accessories, Communications and Fax

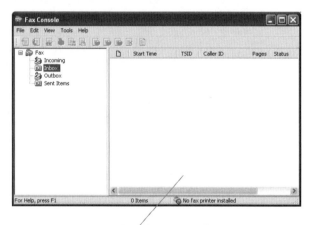

Now you can send and receive faxes with your computer.

Index

W

X

Z